RESTORATION OF THE APOSTOLIC SERIES

APOSTLES

CAN THE CHURCH SURVIVE WITHOUT THEM?

APMI Publications
a division of Kingdom Dimension Books
P.O. Box 17,
55051 Barga (LU),
Tuscany, Italy

RESTORATION OF THE APOSTOLIC SERIES

APOSTLES

CAN THE CHURCH SURVIVE WITHOUT THEM?

DR. ALAN PATEMAN

BOOK TITLE:
Apostles: Can the Church Survive without Them?

This edition published in 2012

Published by APMI Publications
A Division of Kingdom Dimension Books, Library No. **6**
P.O. Box 17,
55051 Barga (LU),
Italy

Email: publications@alanpatemanworldmissions.com
www.AlanPatemanWorldMissions.com

**APMI Publications and Kingdom Dimension Books are a division of
Alan Pateman World Missions**

Printed in the United States of America, Europe and Asia

Paperback ISBN: 978-1-909132-04-7
eBook ISBN: 978-1-909132-05-4

Acknowledgements:
Author/Design/Senior Editor/Publisher: Apostle Dr. Alan Pateman
Editing/Proofreading/Research: Dr. Jennifer Pateman
Computer Administration/Office Manager: Dr. Dorothea Struhlik
Cover Image Credit: © alanpateman

❖

Dedication

I lovingly dedicate this book to my family, especially my wife who is truly gifted. I want to thank them for their love and patience.

Also a big thank you to my administrator Dorothea Struhlik in spending the hours diligently to make sure this book reached publication.

❖

Table of Contents

❖

Introduction

The Bride of Christ, can she handle the strength of her own anointing! Are we fighting the Holy Spirit and not even aware of it...? "Against You, You only, have I sinned" *(Psalm 51:4)*.

Can we contain and understand the season that we are in? Just recently **Billy Brim** was on TV in the UK, she was being interviewed in front of a live audience. They were discussing the anointing of the last days to be poured out upon the Body of Christ before Jesus returns.

Mention was made to the effect that if the Lord had poured out the kind of anointing upon the church that He plans to before Christ is able to return, then it would most certainly have wiped many people out because the church is still not yet adequately prepared. People have to be brought to that place where they can handle the anointing and it not kill them, as in the case of Ananias and Sapphira *(Acts 5:5)*.

People aren't going to get away with some of the things they may have got away with up to now in the church. **The apostolic anointing is currently being restored to the church with the strength of the anointing that existed on the apostles in the early church.** If people come against that anointing they will find themselves fighting the Holy Spirit.

I believe this apostolic move of the end times will restore the true FEAR OF GOD back into the church. To be found fighting, resisting or even lying to almighty God is never good! And when we do find ourselves in that position, we usually cause ourselves much unnecessary harm!

David possessed such revelation, as seen in Psalm 51:4 where he is quoted as saying to the Lord, **"Against thee, thee only, have I sinned"** *(KJV)*. This helps to reveal that when Ananias and his wife *lied,* such sin was not directed against the apostles but against the very person of the Holy Spirit. Just think how many people sin against the Holy Spirit and don't even recognize it!

However in their particular case, I do personally believe that the purity of the Holy Spirit and the wickedness of their own hearts caused such a conflict inside of them that it killed them. They could not stand in the presence of a Holy God and we must understand that this sort of thing may begin happening again, as part of the restoration of the apostolic.

*O worship the LORD in the beauty of holiness: **fear** before him, all the earth.*

(Psalm 96:9 KJV)

There must be **holiness** in the Body of Christ. Jesus is coming back for a bride without spot or wrinkle and without adultery in her heart for the world and her beauty will be as the scripture says, **"...the beauty of Holiness."** While there are *many* unclean spirits in this world, there is only one **HOLY** Spirit!

The nations once again will posses a fear for the children of God, for the **true unadulterated power in the church of the end times.** Just as in the days of the early church, God will display His power through the apostolic ministry. Even though many will be unprepared and not able to handle such an anointing, it MUST be intensified *(the anointing that is)* before Jesus returns.

Billy Brim continued, **"...as much as the anointing is powerful to create, it is as powerfully destructive of evil."** Holiness will show up wickedness in the hearts of men.

Think of it like this: when Jesus turned the water into wine at the wedding feast, what kind of powerful reaction went on inside of those jars *(atomic)* and yet it didn't shatter them! **We as the church have got to be able to contain the anointing without it shattering us!**

Resisting the Anointing

To grieve the Holy Spirit is a serious offense and not something to be taken lightly. Apostles are human vessels chosen by God - capable of making mistakes - but the anointing they carry is sacred. God carefully prepares them and we can see this if we carefully study the lives of Paul and the other apostles.

Many end time apostles are walking the earth again, so dead to self, so yielded to obeying Jesus and so perfected in the love walk that the authority they have is unparalleled. Nations are listening to them because God has granted them a genuine "VOICE" that can be heard.

Apostles are greatly opposed but they have the anointing and the help of the Holy Spirit to handle it. *The world is not worthy of them!* The world reacts to them in every way. They live in a perpetual position of vulnerability and yet of great influence! As we saw with Paul, he was never free of temptation or trials but was a powerfully anointed vessel that carried holy *revelations* directly from almighty God.

In the end times, people will carry such anointing, as we have never seen before. **Many will fail to understand and even become "offended."** The reality is that most people don't know how to recognize true anointing; therefore many will find themselves resisting God in these days!

People found themselves wanting to kill Paul without any concept of who or what he really was. They often rose up in violent opposition against him, but were completely ignorant of the true presence and force of God within him. Everywhere he went somebody or something wanted to kill him! So we must not be surprised at the violent reactions that some people will experience - especially when they come up against this apostolic anointing in the wrong way.

Saying, Touch not mine anointed, and do my prophets no harm.

(1 Chronicles 16:22; Psalm 105:15 KJV)

Introduction

David had a revelation about not touching God's
anointed. Even when tempted to *retaliate,* he always
resisted. When Saul's behaviour was at its worst, David still
recognized the anointing that was upon his king and would
not touch Saul. *(This is a healthy **none-negotiable** for us all!)*

During the famous encounter in the cave that Saul
visited in order to *relieve* himself, David had the perfect
opportunity to kill or capture Saul. He could have said, ***"Oh
Lord... thank you for finally delivering this wretched man
into my hands!"*** Instead David did *not* judge the situation
by the standards of his flesh but by the revelation of God in
his heart, concerning the anointing. Oh how we need this
revelation in the church today.

It's no small thing to be found resisting or grieving the
Holy Spirit. Even though we are heirs of salvation and have
the revelation of Jesus Christ, we must still be found walking
with the Holy Spirit and by His holiness, especially in these
last days!

> *But I say, walk and live [habitually] in the [Holy] Spirit
> [responsive to and controlled and guided by the Spirit];
> then you will certainly not gratify the cravings and desires
> of the flesh [of human nature without God].*
>   *(Galatians 5:16 AMP)*

❖

CHAPTER 1

A Network of Relationships

The Holy Spirit directs us to focus on building "spiritual relationships" so that a strong NET-work can be produced, relationships willing to work together for the purposes of the Kingdom of God.

> *So then, as Christians, do you have any encouragement? Do you have any comfort from love? Do you have any spiritual relationships?* **_Do you have any sympathy and compassion?_** *Then fill me with joy by having the same attitude and the same love, living in harmony, and keeping one purpose in mind.*
>
> *(Philippians 2:1-2 GW)*

Such a network of relationships is *apostolic* in nature and is what the Holy Spirit continues to develop for this ***end time move*** of God. These relationships look for apostolic support and encouragement from other men and women of God in order to move forwards boldly and powerfully in the Holy Spirit; released to fulfil their destinies for the glory of God.

A Network literally means: a linking of people with a common interest or area of concern. Therefore as time develops, we will see a new emphasis on the development of such networks, working together across the board denominationally and via association. Networking does not imply that all groups should come under one "Pope" type figure or one specific apostolic movement.

> *Again, __the kingdom of heaven is like unto a NET__, that was cast into the sea, and gathered of every kind: which, when it was full, they drew to shore, and sat down, and gathered the good into vessels, but cast the bad away.*
> *(Matthew 13:47-48 KJV)*

Instead, Kingdom networking simply involves associations and groups working together, just like large "fishing nets." This can be explained like so: each member of a network represents a single **KNOT** that helps tie the overall net together. In addition, those with the grace, vision and wisdom enough, that is needed to network together with *other* networks - will eventually make up the greater fishing net that God will use to draw in the vast end time harvest of souls. A net that will both be *large enough* and *strong enough* to *catch* and to *hold* such multitudes!

Dr. Bill Hamon says of such networks, *"This gives the Holy Spirit the opportunity to bring a greater unity and corporate vision within the Body of Christ."* This will enable all available resources to be harnessed to work together towards assisting the Body of Christ to initiate and sustain an effective thrust towards souls. *"The common meeting ground is to have the corporate vision of reaping the great end time harvest and proclaiming Jesus Christ as Lord over all the earth" ("Apostles, Prophets and the coming moves of God," p14).*

In the Amplified version of the above scripture, it aptly uses the word DRAGNET: **"Again, the kingdom of heaven is like a <u>dragnet</u> which was cast into the sea and gathered in fish of every sort."** The Message Bible calls it a "fishnet" and the Authorized simply uses the word "net" as above. So the Greek word used for "net" does refer to fishing nets but also to PACKSADDLES, which in the East were simply bags made of *netted-rope.* However perhaps even more interesting is the Greek root meaning for the word "net" used in the Authorized, which means TO EQUIP! *(See Greek #4522 Strong's - also Matthew 4:19; 9:35; 13:49; John 21:1-ff; James 3:13; 4:1-8; 1 Peter 5:5-10).*

Therefore a strong and effective network largely depends upon the people involved *(especially pastors and leaders)* to be totally committed - in every aspect of their lives - to the Lord Jesus Christ. Cheerfully willing to pool their talents and abilities for the "over-all" without begrudging the personal cost.

Such relationships of association through networking are not meant to threaten or contradict denominational loyalties or even cause division; instead they are meant to assist, help bring strength, secure unity and a much greater clarity: especially in enhancing better skills in sharing the Word of God.

One specific aim of a Network is to help establish ministry centres of excellence and influence. Such can be called: *"Spiritually Governmental Hubs,"* that enhance God's Kingdom and provide a significant "platform" *(for all the ministry gifts)* to speak into cities and nations with maximum effectiveness.

Such spiritual hubs help to develop ministries; enhancing and bringing them into positions of leadership that will influence every area of society. Utilizing skills individually and corporately to impact local regions as spheres of influence, for the *Kingdom of God* and the glory of Jesus Christ.

Lastly let's take a look at the significance of knots: we could say that divine appointments are like "knots" in a net. They are **strong-connections** that can take the strain of apostolic relationships! In other words each relationship can be seen as a knot in the overall net. And any net is only as strong as its individual "knots" and "connections!"

Any fisherman will affirm that it's the knots that bring stability to the net and empower the net. Equally true for the Kingdom of God, all of its knots *(divine connections and relationships)* strengthen its net. When such relationships *(knots)* are strong and in place they always breed more of the following: security, prosperity, encouraged abilities, healing, unity, trust and harmony.

> *Behold, how good and how pleasant it is for brethren to* ***dwell together in unity!*** *It is like the precious ointment upon the head, that ran down upon the beard, even Aaron's beard... for there the LORD commanded the blessing...*
> *(Psalm 133:1-3 KJV)*

FACT: Fishermen spend a great portion of their time mending and cleaning their nets; perhaps more time than actually fishing! Likewise we too must spend larger portions of our time securing sound relationships that help develop the net - the Kingdom! Only then will we be more effective.

FACT: Fishing nets can catch vast amounts of fish, with a high percentage of what's caught being thrown directly back into the sea, *(wrong type or size!)* It's a stark reality that many "undesirables" will be caught in the Kingdom's net, that will also be thrown back! **Even God is looking for a certain type of fish - that can be *gutted* correctly!**

In other words, those ready to "give" themselves to the Kingdom are kept and all else are thrown back. Those who are kept in the net *(Kingdom)* are then "CLEANED" and "GUTTED!"

The emphasis in all of this is the "Kingdom of God," as Matthew 13:47 clearly stated; **"the kingdom of heaven is like a net..."** which was a direct teaching about the Kingdom and not just a meagre net! In fact, including this particular parable about the NET, Jesus told **seven short parables** in total, about the Kingdom of God.

1. The Hidden Treasure - Matthew 13:44

2. The Pearl of Great Price - Matthew 13:45-46

3. The Yeast - Matthew 13:33-35, Luke 13:18-19

4. The Mustard Seed -
   Matthew 13:31-32, Mark 4:30-34, Luke 13:18-19

5. The Household Treasures - Matthew 13:52

6. The Sprouting Seed - Mark 4:26-29

7. The Dragnet - Matthew 13:47-50

So based on our knowledge of nets it's been easy to ascertain the basic characteristics of the Kingdom: the restoration of the net equals the healing of relationships. Knots equal the need to submit one to another in effective cooperation and finally anyone who remains in the net *(Kingdom)* will be cleansed and gutted!

Conclusion: the Kingdom of God is only as strong as its relationships *(knots!)* Making DIVINE NETWORKING a *major* part of Kingdom activity. Therefore we must always be ready to work together, safe guarding strong and effective *connections* - with purity of heart - and a willingness to be steered by the larger plan and Kingdom business of the Holy Spirit.

❖

CHAPTER 2

Laying Foundation

Many years ago I was ordained a "bishop" and this is just one of the *titles* that I have gained over the years but I have certainly not chased titles, rather they have chased me! However through the process of my own personal journey I have discovered the importance of such titles, simply because God gave specific gifts to the church and we *must* be able to recognise, *who is who*.

> *Built on the foundation of the apostles and prophets, with Christ Jesus Himself as the chief cornerstone. In Him the whole building is joined together and rises to become* **a holy temple** *in the Lord. And in Him you too are being built together to become a dwelling in which* **God lives by his Spirit**.
>
> *(Ephesians 2:20-22)*

God is not the author of confusion; He knows exactly who he has anointed to serve the purposes, what *gifts* He bestowed on each and exactly how they should operate *(not excluding how others should address or recognise them!)*

Even though many *extremes* exist out there, this is still not reason enough to *totally* dismiss or be in denial about God's gifts for the local church. When we behave like this it is either out of fear or just plain unbelief! In fact many have chosen to *discourage* the use of such titles, based exclusively on their own perceptions and then taught such *perceptions (perceived truths)* to the rest of the Body. But this is not based upon the Word of God, as scripture itself is very clear concerning the correct use of titles.

This means that the very people who attempt to avoid error concerning titles, end up embracing it and then propagating it! All because it feels more *acceptable!* This type of *"replacement theology"* occurs when people literally *"replace"* truth for what allows them to stay within the confines of their own religious comfort zones!

Of course all of us cannot go further than what we have been taught or that which has been revealed to us personally by the Holy Spirit. For example, in the Faith Movement everybody is considered a "pastor!" But in the Evangelical Movement there is a greater emphasis on "eldership" and having a "set" minister.

So generally speaking, there is wide recognition for the pastoral gift, the evangelistic gift and the teacher, but when it comes to the apostle and prophet, they are commonly denied or ignored! People tend to forget that Jesus was indeed our apostle and high priest; with many more titles besides, but not least our *apostle!*

> *Therefore, holy brothers, who share in the heavenly calling, fix your thoughts on* **<u>Jesus, the apostle and high priest</u>** *whom we confess.*
>
> *(Hebrews 3:1)*

I can share from personal experience, that when I travel throughout Europe, it's easier to use the word *apostle* than *bishop!* Yet when I travel throughout the African churches, there is a much greater emphasis on the "bishops," who are held in great esteem, while all others are perceived as being beneath such *hierarchy.*

I would suggest that this is a little backward! Yet I'm not saying we should now throw-the-baby-out-with-the-bath-water and get rid of all the bishops. Not at all! Though correct and balanced teaching *must* be brought back into the church, especially where leadership positions and titles are concerned. Now if the anointing flows *down* and not up, this means that church leaders must get this accurate or the rest of the Body will be confused.

The following is an excerpt concerning the title of bishop, taken from one of my teaching manuals, entitled "The Age of Apostolic Apostleship" *(p58-59).*

Bishop:
There is nothing in this system, which corresponds exactly to the modern diocese episcopate; bishops, when they are mentioned *(Philippians 1:1)* are from

a board of local congregational officers and the position occupied by Timothy and Titus is that of Paul's personal lieutenants in his missionary work. It seems most likely that he was then specially designated with the title of bishop; but even when the monarchical bishop appears in the letters of Ignatius, he is still the pastor of a single congregation.

The word **episkopos** occurs five times in the NT: once of Christ *(1 Peter 2:25)* and in four places of "bishops" or **"overseers" in local churches** *(Acts 20:28; Philippians 1:1; 1 Timothy 3:2, Titus 1:7)*. The verb **episkopeo** occurs in Hebrews 12:15 *("watching")* and *(in some NT MSS)* 1 Peter 5:2 *("exercising the oversight")*.

A bishop then has "oversight of," he is an "overseer." 1 Peter 5:2 says, "Feed the flock of God which is among you, taking the oversight thereof" *(KJV)*. The Greek word for "oversight" is **episkopeo**, Strong's #1983 - to oversee, to beware, to look diligently, take the oversight. Extra words given: direction *(about the times)*, have charge of, take aim at *(spy)*, regard, consider, take heed, look at *(on)*, mark.

Take for instance when I was on a ministry trip recently in Africa, I was asked to be involved in a *presbytery,* during a particular ordination service, *(some of those individuals to be ordained that day, I might add, were accomplished men in their own right, one in particular was acting chaplain to a very high-ranking government official within his own country and was held in high regard himself).*

However during the process of this extremely ceremonial meeting, they proceeded to make such a fan fare of these prospective bishops, to the point that it was almost ridiculous! The last person they ordained that day was a woman evangelist, whom they ordained an apostle and whom they gave very little prominence to at all. They clearly misunderstood the *governing role* and *office* of an apostle, versus the general *overseeing role* of a bishop, *(I had the unpleasant job of trying to straighten out their theology before I left).*

However we cannot allow *confusion* to reign unchallenged, in the Body of Christ, especially concerning such important matters as these and thus fuels my passion even more, to help *restore* some clarity back into the church, about the true position, nature and role of the apostle; in regards to the other five-fold-ministry gifts, as well as putting the record straight about "bishops" who were originally and basically commissioned as "overseers" for the local-church!

Only by turning to scripture can we reveal the true *position-that-goes-with-the-title* and show up whether or not certain "replacement doctrine" has crept into the church. Again, once error is embraced, it readily circulates throughout the rest of the Body like a virus that must be stopped and corrected!

It's important for us to realise that we are currently in the move of the apostolic and the prophetic - so let's define the gift of *apostle* in particular and whether such a gift truly exists today! **Please at this point - don't decide that titles do not matter, they do have their place, even today!**

Consider Paul in whose writings he often declared himself, "Paul an apostle." Why? Because Paul knew exactly who he was and what he was commissioned to do. This should be true of the rest of us, because there is clear foundation and structure to the Body of Christ, which Jesus Himself put into place.

Let's look at the following 5 objectives:

1). The First Objective of an Apostle: "By the grace God has given me, I laid a foundation as an expert builder, and someone else is building on it. But each one should be careful how he builds..." *(1 Corinthians 3:10) Strong's #753 architekton (ar-khee-tek'-tone); from 746 and 5045; a chief constructor, i.e. architect, KJV - **masterbuilder.***

Superintendent: he is more than just an architect; He is like a "superintendent" of the building process. *Strong's #5045 tekton (tek'-tone); from the base of 5098: an artificer (as producer of fabrics), i.e. (specifically) a **craftsman** in wood: KJV - carpenter.*

This apostolic function is the necessary basis for every local church, which forms part of the household of God. "Consequently, you are no longer foreigners and aliens, but fellow citizens with God's people and members of God's household, built on the foundations of the apostles and prophets, with Christ Jesus Himself as the chief cornerstone" *(Ephesians 2:19-20).*

2). He Lays a Foundation of Life in Christ:

By the grace God has given me, I laid a foundation as an expert builder, and someone else is building on it. But

*each one should be careful how he builds. For no one can
lay any foundation other than the one already laid, which
is Jesus Christ.*

(1 Corinthians 3:10)

This is done very importantly via the Word of truth
but also by fatherly relationship. In other words, it's not
just achieved by endless *impersonal* teachings; "For though
ye have one thousand instructors in Christ, yet have ye not
many <u>fathers:</u> for in Christ Jesus I have begotten you through
the gospel" *(1 Corinthians 4:15 KJV).*

Note: speakers only have *hearers,* **where fathers have**
children! A father-in-the-faith is not a remote and austere
figure that separates himself from the people but is *real* and
approachable, just as a father with his son.

However even though an apostle takes on that fatherly
role, another major emphasis must be established here, that
an apostle is a **BUILD-ER** and not just a **BLESS-ER!** For
example he is not easily given to emotions and shallow-short-
term-solutions, *(which are often miss-represented as "blessing!")*

No! He is in it for the *long-term* and is willing to go the
extra mile with people, in order to *build* something
substantial into their lives. In other words, an apostle is
never committed to the popular **"hit-n-run"** or **"quick-fix"**
solutions, but sticks with the process until he sees real
fruit appear in peoples lives! **"My dear children, for
whom I am again in the pains of childbirth** *until* **Christ
is formed in you..."** *(Galatians 4:19)*

3). He Lays a Foundation of Obedience towards Christ: he stresses clearly from the beginning the Lordship of Jesus Christ for whom he is pledged to make disciples. He aims to bring about the "obedience of faith" and looks for that obedience to be complete.

> *Through him and for his name's sake, we received grace and apostleship to call people from among all the Gentiles to the obedience that comes from faith.*
>
> *(Romans 1:5)*

One definite fact is that it's hard to get away with *anything,* **when an apostle is around!** His aim is to help each individual in the church to build his house upon the only sure foundation of obedience - the commandments of Jesus.

> *Then Jesus came to them and said, "All authority in heaven and on earth has been given to me. Therefore go and make disciples of all nations, baptizing them in the name of the Father and of the Son and of the Holy Spirit, and teaching them to obey everything **I have commanded** you. And surely I am with you always, to the very end of the age."*
>
> *(Matthew 28:18-20)*

> *Therefore everyone who hears these words of mine and puts them into practice is like a wise man who **built his house** on the rock...*
>
> *(Matthew 7:24)*

4). He Lays a Foundation of Doctrine: before the church can go on to maturity, the foundational doctrine must have been clearly laid. This is the responsibility of the apostle. To build and to work, making sure that every member of the church is clear on repentance and faith, baptism in water and the Holy Spirit; on eternal judgment and the resurrection from the dead.

> *Therefore let us leave the elementary teachings about Christ and go on to **maturity**, not laying again the foundation of repentance from acts that lead to death, and of faith in God, instructions about baptisms, the laying on of hands, the resurrection of the dead, and eternal judgment. And God permitting, we will do so.*
>
> *(Hebrews 6:1-3)*

He will establish them on the same sure foundation of their death and resurrection with Christ.

> *So then, just as you received Christ Jesus as Lord, continue to live in Him, rooted and **built up in Him**, strengthened in faith as you were taught, and overflowing with thankfulness.*
>
> *(Colossians 2:6-7)*

He confirms in them the dynamic of what it means to be united with Christ *(Romans 6:1ff)*. He contends with every error and distortion that would detract from the fullness of Jesus and diminish the believer's fullest experience of Him.

> *See to it that no-one takes you captive through hollow and deceptive philosophy, which depends on human tradition and the basic principles of this world rather than on Christ. For in Christ all the fullness of the Deity lives in bodily form, and you have been given fullness in Christ, who is the Head over every power and authority.*
>
> *(Colossians 2:8-10)*

Legalism, asceticism, mysticism and pseudo-spirituality are all refuted and corrected. The Word of God is for the apostle, the *only* existing basis for building.

5). The "master-builder" is responsible for the whole construction and supervises the entire work. He is especially concerned for the fitting-out of the building for its intended use. A house must be finished so that the occupants can take up residence.

An apostolic leader is equally concerned for the house of God. He sees that the parts of the building are fitted and equipped to serve their function. All this is so that the church may once more be a dwelling place fit for God and his Holy Spirit *(Ephesians 2:20)*.

❖

CHAPTER 3

Types of Apostles

In this particular chapter we are going to clearly differentiate between the two *major* types of apostles *(as there are others, such as "regional" apostles and so forth)*. However to begin with the word apostle means: "to-send-forth;" someone with a commission to fulfil; representing the same authority that sent them.

> *Paul, an apostle - **sent** not from men nor by man, but by Jesus Christ and God the Father, who raised him from the dead...*
>
> *(Galatians 1:1)*

We see this in the following scriptures; "Jesus said to them, 'If God were your Father, you would love me, for I came from God and now am here. I have not come on my own; but He <u>sent</u> me...'" *(John 8:42)* "Because of this, God in his wisdom said, 'I will send them prophets and apostles, some of whom they will kill and others they will persecute'" *(Luke 11:49)*. "Again Jesus said, 'Peace be with you! As the Father has sent me, I am sending you'" *(John 20:21)*.

Therefore an "apostle" is not someone who is sent by men or appointed by men, but by God. Again we go straight to scripture in order to see this; "Paul, an apostle - <u>sent</u> not from men nor by man, but by Jesus Christ and God the Father, who raised him from the dead..." *(Galatians 1:1)* "Paul called to be an apostle of Christ Jesus by the will of God..." *(1 Corinthians 1:1)* "He who receives you receives me, and he who receives me receives the one who sent me..." *(Matthew 10:40 - see also Acts 14:14; 15:23; Romans 16:7; 2 Corinthians 8:23; 1 Thessalonians 1:1)*

Now before I go any further, let me add to this by taking an excerpt from one of Ulf Ekman's books called, **"The Apostolic Ministry"** *(p20-21)*.

"Apostles and prophets lay the foundation for the church: This century has seen increasing revelation on the ministry gifts. We have begun to understand what a pastor is, how an evangelist functions and what a teacher does. However, there are two special gifts that we need to understand so that God can develop strong local churches in the Last Days.

There is a fierce struggle concerning these gifts going on right now across the earth. The devil hates strong churches. He tries to crush them, tear them down and render them passive and ineffective. If he can remove the gifts that develop strong local churches, then he'll be satisfied. Apostles and prophets are the gifts that do this more than any other.

<u>*The apostle and the prophet are like spearheads, and the church is built on the foundation they lay*</u> *(Ephesians 2:20). If they are not allowed to lay a proper foundation, then the church will lose direction, strength, anointing and spiritual insight. You can have good meetings, interesting conferences and fantastic campaigns without these gifts. But when the preachers leave and the crowds disappear, where is the strength that's needed for the local church? If you look closely, you'll see that the church is small, exhausted, confused and unsure of its direction.*

The apostle and the prophet, especially the apostle, channel strength to the churches that helps them grow on a daily basis. **Churches are not built on conferences, campaigns and seminars. They are built by the steady labour of ordinary people, who are constantly developing and maturing.** *Maturity, in a biblical sense, refers to increased vigour and stability, which makes us stronger. The apostle's ministry is vital and the bible gives us many examples of this."*

Therefore it is important that we have a balanced concept of what an apostle is and what an apostle is really sent to do. Otherwise *(and just as I have witnessed around the world)*, this authentic and much needed role of the apostle is "misunderstood" and is desperately "lacking" within the church.

Often it is misconstrued as something intolerable, domineering and threatening. However in reality it couldn't be further from the truth and totally robs the church of a vital element that will help it to grow strong and STAY strong! So instead of complaining about all the weaknesses in the church we must allow the apostle to take back his rightful position in the Body of Christ. Only then can we witness, the kind of power, strength, authority and single-mindedness of the early church that we all crave to see.

The devil fears this kind of strength and will do anything to uphold the myth that apostles *(and prophets)* are obsolete and no longer necessary. The devil IS a liar! Oh how we need the apostolic ministry today and how little will be achieved without it.

However in order for the church to be of significance once again, we need the apostolic ministry to do what it was sent *forth* to do. To bring: stability, maturity and growth.

None of us want to create works that have no substance. Puff pastry looks substantial on the outside but once you break through its veneer and crust there is no substance underneath! It looks impressive and glazed sitting up top but has little *(if any)* foundation. Spiritual puff pastry is a far cry from what God has planned for His church and for that which Christ died.

Resurrection Apostles

Now let's differentiate between the following types of apostles: **the resurrection and ascension apostles.** The original twelve *(minus Judas)* make up the first group, as they were directly commissioned by Jesus and received the inbreathing of resurrection life directly from Him, *(as the first fruits of His new creation)*.

From Jesus they received proof of His being alive and the principles of His Kingdom first hand. And once reinforced by Matthias *(Acts 1:12f)* they received the promised Holy Spirit at Pentecost. They are also known as the APOSTLES OF THE LAMB. "The wall of the city had twelve foundations, and on them were the names of the twelve apostles of the Lamb" *(Revelations 21:14)*.

Furthermore Paul must be included in this particular group of apostles for the reason we see here, **"...and last of all he appeared to me also, as one abnormally born"** *(1 Corinthians 15:8)*. And it is the testimony of this exclusive group of men that forms the definitive standard of teaching and doctrine for us. For example, we believe Jesus through *their* word, in the context of what Jesus spoke here in John 17:20, **"My prayer is not for them alone, I pray also for those who will believe in me through <u>their</u> message..."**

Strictly speaking *(concerning "resurrection apostles")* their only true successor is the New Testament itself; which preserves the record of their inspired testimony.

> *I have much more to say to you, more than you can now bear. But when he, the Spirit of truth, comes; he will guide you into all truth. He will not speak on His own; he will speak only what he hears, and he will tell you what is yet to come. He will bring glory to me by taking from what is mine and making it known to you...*
>
> *(John 16:12-14)*

All subsequent apostolic ministries *("ascension apostles")* must *submit to* and *accurately reflect* their testimony. It can be said like this; the words of the "resurrection apostles" are still primary and still scripture; but however, any other apostolic word is only *derivative (non-scripture).*

Unfortunately this is just where some of our modern-day apostles *(recent-past and present)* have made their errors. Some of them have wrongly imagined that this status of being an "apostle" gave their own words the same footing and weight as scripture itself! Clearly mistaken they have misunderstood their proper boundaries.

To be clear about this, no one today is receiving any "additional revelation" that can add or take away from the original foundation of the gospel. We already have the revelation of the New Testament. Paul said, **"But though we, or an angel from heaven, preach any other gospel unto you than that, which we have preached unto you, let him be accursed"** *(Galatians 1:8 KJV).* Paul warned that we are to take heed how we build upon the foundation that has already been laid *(1 Corinthians 3:10).* Quite simply we can't add to it or take *anything* away from it.

Ascension Apostles

As mentioned already above, there exists a clear distinction between these two sets of apostles, those of the resurrection *(apostles of the Lamb)* and those of the ascension. In addition to this fact and to further explain this, it can be said that Paul was very much a "pivot" in that he was not only the last of the resurrection apostles *(who actually saw the risen Lord Jesus Christ)* but was also the first of a new series of apostles, called the **ascension apostles.**

To appreciate another *(ascension)* apostle, I turn again to the writings of Ulf Ekman and insert a paragraph from his book: **"The Apostolic Ministry - can the Church Live without It?"** *(p23)*

> *"The Apostolic Ministry has Long-term Effects: we must be set free from the idea of a religious 'St Paul' as portrayed in marble statues, icons and ancient historical images. We must see him in the unique role he had. It was Paul who received the revelation of Jesus' resurrection and wrote one-third of the New Testament. He remains the most important example of a Christian today after Jesus - our primary example.*
>
> *Paul is an example in two areas: first he shows us how a Christian should live… lives of consistency. Second, he exemplifies the ministry of an apostle. He demonstrates the function of an apostle and the results that follow… Every ministry gift operates within the restrictions of time. The ministry of John the Baptist was effective for only a short period of time, yet his influence was great. Paul not only affected his era, but his influence has remained from generation to generation up to our present day.*
>
> *An examination of the apostolic ministry will show that its influence continues even after the apostle has died. History speaks of men who weren't called apostles but were in fact just that. Wycliffe was definitely an apostle,*

as his degree of influence demonstrates. Huss, Luther, Calvin, Knox and Wesley were also apostles. How do we know? From their preaching, their message, their ministry and the enduring legacy they left behind. These are some of the signs of the apostle."

Yes! The apostle is certainly in it for *long haul* and not even his natural death can limit his influence. That's exciting! But there is much more to an apostle than this, we have only discussed *some* of the signs of an apostle - there is more.

In closing this particular chapter let me summarize by clearly saying, that not all apostles were like Paul. Some had lesser and some greater anointing, including different gifting. But the fact remains; there are two distinct categories of apostles: those of the resurrection and those of the ascension. Today apostles are still *commissioned* and *sent-forth,* and still possess great influence. Even today we can refer to them as **ascension apostles.**

❖

CHAPTER 4

Marks of an Apostle

In our last chapter we defined the difference between resurrection and ascension apostles. We looked at the basic meaning of the word apostle as being "sent-forth" by God. In this chapter we proceed by discussing the major *functions* and *characteristics* of an apostle.

The things that mark an apostle - signs, wonders and miracles - were done among you with great perseverance.
(2 Corinthians 12:12)

There are clear elements that dominate the calling and gifting of an apostle; which causes all apostles to act in similar ways. In other words, they can be very different in personality and background, but their gifting will have similar functions and boundaries. Firstly and arguably the most important is that apostles are very good at *working-together*, whereas other gifts are more prone to being *competitive!* Although a true apostle will not build on the foundation of another *(usurp)*, he will always allow other apostles to work together *with* him, in the spirit of relationship and collaboration.

In fact I would say that this is one of the *quickest* ways of detecting whether someone is an authentic apostle or not! **True apostles will work together.** Those who compete and clamber over others to "get-ahead," are ruthless like businessmen, *not* apostles. **Apostles do NOT compete.**

Instead they have a unique understanding about foundations and just how *counter-productive* it can be to build upon the foundation that another has laid, and to usurp the authority of another. He will not waste his time. He would rather work in *conjunction with* or go somewhere else and lay down a whole new foundation!

Another feature or characteristic of the apostle is that of a PIONEER. They go first. When scripture said, **"...first apostles"** in 1 Corinthians 12:28, this was *not* just a sentiment of hierarchy but literally meant that apostles would *go-first, in front and pioneer!*

They break-open new ground and are not at all shy of ploughing where it has never been ploughed before. Nor do they shy away from *hard work.* **In fact you have never known real hard work until you have been around a true apostle** *(ask those who know!)* Their work ethic is second to none and they have *durability* and *spiritual backbone* that others even half their age can lack!

Their ability to endure hardship is another trait of the apostle. They are not fragile or delicate in their approach; they can be tough at times, yet remain loving and fatherly. They will observe and watch maturely, while others race and chase opportunities. They possess unequalled wisdom with a *panoramic scope* of view that keeps track on the pulse of where everything's up to, in the overall development of things!

This is unique to the apostle. Whose spiritual scope and sight is much more *far reaching* than the other gifts of the Body. Even though the prophet is considered the "seer," it is the role of the apostle to over-see the wider production and development of God's Kingdom. This is why the prophet and apostle need each other and must work closely together - including the other gifts.

Apostles can have different gift mixtures, such as an apostle who is a pastor or an apostle who is a teacher and so forth. Still, regardless of gifting, we see during many different instances throughout scripture, how the apostles would work *together.*

One example for this is found in Acts 2:42 where it says; **"They devoted themselves to the _apostles'_ teaching... to the breaking of bread and to prayer."** Notice how the plural was used - **"apostle-s"** - showing that more than one apostle was involved in teaching those people.

Authentic apostles do not get caught up with the fame-game. In fact they are not driven by the need for fame, rather their need for **accomplishment!** Apostles are productive wherever they are, just as Paul was never found *stifled* by circumstance. Even when left to languish in prison for a season or discovered under house arrest Paul wrote some of his best works during those specific periods. **Nothing deterred him from his mission and nothing could chain down his revelation.** In fact hardship helped propel it!

In addition to all of this, apostles are not generally nervous about money - the abundance or lack of it! Scripture shows that Paul was very robust, knowing how to abase or abound. Whatever the situation *(or season)* called for, he was willing. And not just for the sake of proving how robust he could be, but for the furtherance of the gospel and advancement of the cause.

So apostles are ready for just about anything and regular variations of season do not shake them, they just live prepared. All of which is another characteristic of an apostle. Apart from being extremely hard working and focused, they have a deep appreciation for "PREPARATION." They are always preparing, which is why they are always prepared. THEY LIVE PREPARED!

An apostle who does not feel *prepared* is generally not a happy apostle. This is when he can get a little gruff! It is also why you will never find an apostle sitting around doing nothing *(even in his sleep he is building or preparing **something!**)*

Sturdy is equal to "nerdy" in the world's eyes, but for an apostle **spiritual-backbone** is everything. One of their greatest satisfactions is derived from seeing "spiritual-maturity" outworked in the people. To help people *realize* and *release* the gifting that is within them.

In short, an apostle will always stir up the saints for ACTION and bring an explosion of life and activity wherever they are. *(Whether it's a good or bad reaction that's stirred, there's **always** a re-action around an apostle).*

So being lazy is a luxury around an apostle! No one gets away with it! They are hard wired to motivate people and therefore no one feels comfortable doing *nothing* around them! *(They can make even a hardened and self-confessed workaholic feel lazy!)*

However, it's all taken in their stride, by the inspiration of the Holy Spirit and each apostle possesses a specific *time-frame* to work in. They are uniquely aware of "time" and hate to waste it, working tirelessly to achieve the goals set before them. *(Note: seasoned apostles don't tire with age because they have grown in wisdom and therefore also in their ability to **delegate** - most apostles could put an army to work, quite easily!)*

Nothing displeases them more than to see rampant apostasy amongst God's people and spiritual carelessness or sloppiness. Therefore it's also good to point out that the apostle is not heavily prone to taking spiritual short cuts. No architect would do it. The safety of their overall structure would be compromised and the apostle sees things much the same way!

Another characteristic is ORDER; the apostle has an affinity with all-things-order. They generally bring order into chaos and restoration where there is brokenness. They are the ones trusted with God's blue print, as they are God's builders. Likewise, just as Nehemiah discovered he must remove the rubbish-heap before he could proceed building the walls of Jerusalem, an apostle will equally deal with the chaos that tries to hinder God's plan *(Nehemiah 1-3)*.

In fact no other gift can maintain the level of order that an apostle can effectuate *(put into force or operation)*. By his powers of delegation and skills of origination, he deals with any chaos *(naturally or spiritually speaking)* within his given sphere of influence and looks to permanently remove any obstacles that threaten to hinder or delay the successful completion of God's design.

Eight points to Remember

1). Plurality - apostles work as part of a team *(1 Thessalonians 1:1; 2:6):* Let's look a little deeper at the apostle's ability to work alone but also as part of a team. He is not easily threatened and likes to work with others. In fact over "twenty men," at one time or another, were associated with Paul in his apostolic travels. **True apostles are not charismatic lone-rangers** who lack and even despise the checks and balances of plurality. This is one reason that they like to bring on younger men in their calling in God, such as Paul did with Timothy.

2). Gifts and anointing *(1 Thessalonians 1:5a):* they have spiritual "power" not just ecclesiastical "status." **They enjoy the charisma of the Holy Spirit rather than their ordination papers** or may not even be officially ordained by a denomination.

God is rising up a new breed of apostolic ministers who will readily admit that they are embryonic and earnestly desire and covet the wonders and miracles that are one of the signs of a true apostle. **"The things that mark an apostle - signs, wonders and miracles - were done among you with great perseverance"** *(2 Corinthians 12:12)*.

3). Has a proven character *(1 Thessalonians 1:5b)*: we see in scripture that the apostles were men of integrity with mastery over wrong motives. For example they were not out to deceive, flatter or make money from those they ministered to *(1 Thessalonians 2:2-6),* men worthy of imitating.

4). Is a man of patience and gentleness *(1 Thessalonians 2:6-7):* because he is a man of faith he can afford to wait. Because he is a man of love he does not have to throw his weight about. **Building with living bricks takes time and trouble.** Taking another look at the sign of a true apostle, *(2 Corinthians 12:12)* we find the word **perseverance** *(patience KJV)*.

This reveals that true apostles are not mere remote office managers presiding over some new charismatic empire, which they lay claim to "covering." True apostles are prepared to spend time with individuals and not *just* leaders at that *(unless one is called to leaders specifically)*. They are *"on-site"* superintendents of the work.

5). A Bearer of God's Word *(1 Thessalonians 2: 13):* "And for this purpose I was appointed a herald and an apostle - I am telling the truth, I am not lying - and a teacher of the true faith to the Gentiles" *(1 Timothy 2:7)*. No man can ultimately be recognised as an apostle, who does not have a proven ministry as a preacher and a teacher of the Word of God, for it is that which is the root of his authority, the source of his life and the dynamic of his ministry, he is a preacher and teacher of the Word *before* he is an apostle.

6). He stands or falls by the church *(1 Thessalonians 1:6-7):* Like Peter, he should have been a fellow-elder in a local Body. There, he can be tested and checked as he learns like everybody else, what it is to submit to one another in the fear of the Lord. As a local elder, he knows the responsibility of rule and pastoral care, which leaders in the church have, and then as an apostle, will be able to speak into other churches with greater sensitivity.

> *To the elders among you, I appeal as a fellow-elder, a witness to Christ's sufferings and one who also will share in the glory to be revealed: Be shepherds of God's flock that is under your care, **serving** as overseers - not because you must, but because you are willing, as God wants you to be; not greedy for money, but eager to serve...*
>
> *(1 Peter 5:1-2)*

7). One who is "sent-out" by the church to which he belongs, an apostle carries credibility with him. Those who receive him can expect that he will have worked out *(learnt)* at home whatever he is laying on them as counsel; in this way Paul and Barnabas were "released" by the church at Antioch *(Acts 13:1-3).*

Being sent out by the church of which they were a part - they are eager to return to give their support and report.

From Attalia they sailed back to Antioch, where they had been committed to the grace of God for the work they had now completed. On arriving there, they gathered the church together and reported all that God had done through them and how he had opened the door of faith to the Gentiles.

(Acts 14:26-27)

8). Finally and most importantly true apostles appreciate being "accountable." This gives them a sense of security, saves them from the wrong kind of independence and reminds them they exist to serve the Body and not themselves. They desire the best for the church *(1 Thessalonians 2:19)*.

❖

CHAPTER 5

Are there Apostles Today?

Much of what is in this current book has been taken from my articles called, "Truth for the Journey." Many across the Internet enjoy these articles; likewise we enjoy the tremendous feedback and positive responses they provoke!

In particular, an apostle who lives in Spain called, "Emilio Sevilla" dropped me a line to encourage but also to elaborate a little deeper on the meaning of the word apostle. I quote him: "The word apostle means *'sent-to-establish'* because the word is made up of two words which are, APO-STELLO - APO means to be sent forth and STELLO means to establish… this is why apostles should not rest until they have established the Kingdom in their given area…" End quote.

To see this in its various forms, we simply go to the Strong's Greek Concordance. To do so we take the precise place in scripture where Paul emphatically introduces himself as an "apostle" in his letter to the Corinthians, "Paul, called **to be** an apostle of Jesus Christ through the will of God..." *(1 Corinthians 1:1 KJV)* or as the Young's Literal Translation puts it, "Paul, a called *apostle* of Jesus Christ..."

The Greek word that was used here is the compound word apostolos: *(ap-os'-tol-os 00652)* specifically meaning; a delegate; specially, an ambassador of the Gospel; officially a commissioner of Christ *("apostle") (with miraculous powers):* --apostle, messenger, **he that is sent.** However there are actually numerous compound words that help make up or have influence upon the meaning of this word apostle - which we have all become familiar with.

For sure, the more we see what apostles do, the more we realise how indispensable their ministry is. The Acts of the Apostles is a book with no ending, as it records that which Jesus began to do and teach; He continues to do and say through His apostles; apostolic men who have the ability to father the church, its pastors and people. They are blessings from God, so much needed for today.

Yet there are still those who ask, **"Are there apostles for today?"** Of course the answer has to be an unequivocal "Yes!" But let us qualify this answer because there are many who would answer, "No." To those who still question the validity of apostleship for today I would say that if there are prophets, evangelists, pastors and teachers then there must be apostles too.

Why? Because Jesus Himself gave and commissioned **all five** of these gifts to His bride and as long as this institution that we call church remains upon the earth - until Christ returns for it - then these five gifts will remain in full!

As stated before, apostles willingly work together just as the twelve did in the beginning, to lay the foundation for the very first church in Jerusalem. However were they really "unique" as some like to suggest, in an attempt to imply that apostles had their rightful place in the beginning, but are *obsolete* for today.

"Unique?" Yes, in the context that only they walked with Christ from the time of His baptism by John the Baptist, until He rose from the dead. They were also eyewitnesses of all that Jesus said and did. Some of them even recorded what they experienced *(testimony)*, which became part of the New Testament that we have and love today. In addition they not only received divine revelation, but also communicated that revelation *once and for all*. Yet even with this fact in place, the bible *never* stipulated that these were the first and final *(only)* apostles for the church.

The most prominent apostles of all were Peter and Paul and arguably that the most important was Paul - who was not even among the original twelve, yet neither was Barnabas who we also found being called an apostle in scripture *(see Acts 14:14-15)*. This is the point. Scripture clearly states that they were both apostles. Furthermore, we find in Galatians 1:19 that James the brother of Jesus was also considered an "apostle."

In addition to this we find Paul writing about the apostolic ministry of Silvanus and Timothy *(who incidentally were also not part of the original twelve)* in his letter to the Philippians and there exists many more examples of this in scripture. So it appears there were indeed many more apostles that the bible identifies - outside of the original twelve! They even lived and functioned during the same lifetime as the original twelve but were not included into that band. This identifies that the apostolic ministry was in circulation and was not limited to a certain number.

So the purpose of the apostles for the early church was clear. They helped lay the foundations and continued to establish and build upon what Christ had said and done. With this in mind then, let us ask the following question regarding today's church:

- **Is the building finished?**
- **Is the bride ready?**
- **Is the church full-grown and are the saints completely equipped?**
- **Has the church attained its ordained maturity and unity?**

I dare say this: only when the answer to these few questions is a **"YES,"** can we dispense with the apostolic ministry.

❖

CHAPTER 6

The Apostolic Ministry functions Today

S o we are slowly establishing the fact, using scripture to qualify, that the apostolic ministry was indeed something that Christ ordained Himself and is still in function today.

For the same God who worked through Peter as the apostle to the Jews also worked through me as the apostle to the Gentiles.

(Galatians 2:8 NLT)

Now in order for such apostolic ministry to function correctly and be at its best *(as God intended and not as man-made hierarchy prefers it)*, we must be "in-charge-of-our-egos" especially where clerical *titles* are concerned! Even though Christ Himself gave such gifts their titles, we must not think of ourselves more highly than we aught *(Romans 12:3)*.

Consider that in addition to holding-office, the apostle is also a ministry-gift to the Body; nevertheless he is first a **SERVANT,** as are *all* the other gifts/offices that Christ ordained.

It is undeniable that Satan will try and destroy the anointed "structure" that God is restoring through His apostolic ministries. Satan knows full well that a house in division against itself *(against its own ordained structure)* will collapse. He capitalizes on this by triggering some of the "in-fighting" that exists between the different "gifts" in the Body, *(making them totally counter-productive).*

Individual gifts are deceived very effectively when simply steered down wrong paths *(that are not ordained for them).* Let's be honest, a little "steering" here and there, is all it takes to make even the most "sincere" amongst us, totally ineffective! In other words our adversary might not be able to influence our love for Christ or dampen our zeal but he certainly can and does influence our egos, time and time again!

All apostolic ministries must never forget that they have been called to serve the church and not their own egos! Whenever power is involved, this can prove challenging *(1 Peter 5:5-8).*

It's important to look at the apostle in relation to the other apostolic gifts. By way of a simple illustration, take the hand and imagine each of the fingers to represent one of the five fold ministry gifts that Christ gave to His Body.

• **The index finger:** represents the prophet - the one who points the way and says just like Isaiah "This is the way; walk in it…" *(30:21)* Therefore he gives direction, tells of the spiritual condition of the church and exposes its sin!

• **The middle finger:** represents the evangelist. His ministry is more widespread than others. He reaches further. He is stifled if left in the confines of the church. He loves to be out in the field. He needs to be let loose to do his job, supported and equipped by the church that sends him out - to go beyond its confines and be effective.

• **The ring finger:** represents the pastor's ministry. He is totally committed to his flock - loving as a shepherd would - caring, encouraging and meeting the individual needs of his sheep.

• **The little finger:** represents the teacher's ministry - the finger small enough to clear away the wax in the ears so that folks can hear well and understand better!

• **Lastly the thumb:** represents the apostle. It is sturdier than the other fingers and can touch all of the others with ease! This implies that an apostle can function in all of the other ministry gifts - when necessary. He brings stability and flexibility, which is essential for the Body to grow with strength and maturity.

However and perhaps most importantly is the fact that without a thumb it is impossible to "grasp" anything. **In fact only when the other fingers cooperate with the thumb - can the job get done!**

It's elementary then, that just as the fingers of one hand must work together, so too must apostolic ministries cooperate and collaborate together so that they can be of benefit to the Body that they are called to.

Apostolic Gifts flowing Together

In his book, "Apostles, Prophets and the coming moves of God" Dr. Bill Hamon brings out the following:

"**Fivefold Ministries:** These are the fivefold ascension gift ministries as revealed in Ephesians 4:11 - apostle, prophet, evangelist, pastor and teacher. They are not gifts of the Holy Spirit per se, but an extension of Christ's headship ministry to the church. Their primary ministry and function are to teach, train, activate and mature the saints for the work of their ministries *(Ephesians 4:12-13).*

• **Apostle:** one of the fivefold ministries of Ephesians 4:11. The apostle is a foundation-laying ministry *(Ephesians 2:20)* that we see in the New Testament establishing new churches *(Paul's missionary journeys)*, correcting error by establishing proper order and structure *(first epistle to the Corinthians)*, and acting as an oversight ministry that fathers other ministries *(1 Corinthians 4:15; 2 Corinthians 11:28).*

The New Testament apostle has a revelatory anointing *(Ephesians 3:5)*. Some major characteristics are **great patience** and manifestations of **signs, wonders and miracles.** We will know more and see greater manifestations concerning the apostle during the peak of the apostolic movement.

• **Prophet:** He is a man of God whom Christ has given the ascension gift of a 'prophet' *(Ephesians 4:11; 1 Corinthians 12:28; 14:29; Acts 11:27; 13:1)*. A prophet is one of the fivefold ascension gift ministers who are an extension of Christ's ministry to the church. He is an anointed minister who has the gifted ability to perceive and to speak the specific mind of Christ to individuals, churches, businesses and nations.

Greek: 'prophetes' *(prof-ay-tace)* a foreteller, an inspired speaker *(Strong's Concordance,Vine's Concordance)*. A proclaimer of a divine message, denoted among the Greeks as an interpreter of the oracles of gods.

In the Septuagint it is the translation of the word 'roeh' - a seer - indicating that the prophet was one who had immediate intercourse with God *(1 Samuel 9:9)*. It also translates the word 'nabhi,' meaning either, *'one in whom the message from God springs forth, or one to whom anything is secretly communicated' (Amos 3:7; Ephesians 3:5)*.

• **Prophetess:** Greek 'prophetis' - the feminine of prophet *(Gk. Prophetes)*. A woman of God whom the Holy Spirit has given the divine prophetic ability to perceive and speak the mind of Christ on specific matters to particular people. Strong's - a *'female foreteller or an inspired woman.'* She is a specially called woman who functions like the New Testament prophet to minister to the Body of Christ with inspired speaking and prophetic utterance *(Acts 2:17; 21:9; Luke 2:36; Isaiah 8:3; 2 Chronicles 34:22; Jude 4; Exodus 15:20)*.

Prophetess is the proper title for a woman with this ascension gift and calling. **Prophet** is the proper title for a man with this ascension gift and calling.

• **Evangelist:** The traditional view of the evangelist is a bearer of the *'Good News,'* proclaiming the gospel to the unbelieving world; exemplified by modern-day evangelists who preach the message of salvation in crusades and the like. However, Philip, the New Testament evangelist mentioned in Acts 21:8, demonstrated a strong supernatural dimension to the evangelistic ministry.

Philip preached the gospel to the lost *(Acts 8:5),* moved in miracles *(8:6),* delivered people from demons *(8:7),* received instructions from an angel *(8:26),* had revelation knowledge *(8:29),* and was supernaturally translated from Gaza to Asotus *(8:26, 40).* We are looking forward to the restoration of this type of prophetic evangelist to the Body of Christ.

• **Pastor:** 'Poiment, a shepherd, one who tends herds or flocks *(not merely one who feeds them),* is used metaphorically of Christian pastors.' Episkopeo *(overseer, bishop)* is an overseer, and Pesbuteros *(elder)* is another term for the same person as bishop or overseer. They normally give the title to the senior minister of the local church, regardless of his fivefold calling. It is a shepherding ministry to feed and care for the flock.

Responsibilities that appear connected with the pastoral ministry include oversight and care of the saints, providing spiritual food for their growth and development, leadership and guidance, and counsel. Prophetic pastors not only do the things normally associated with pastoring, but also move in supernatural graces and gifts of God *(prophesying, word of knowledge, healing)* and have the vision and willingness to develop the saints in their gifts and callings.

• **Teacher:** An instructor of truth. *'All scripture is given by inspiration of God, and is profitable for doctrine, for reproof, for correction, for instruction in righteousness' (2 Timothy 3:16 KJV).* A New Testament apostolic-prophetic teacher is one who not only teaches the letter of the Word, but also ministers with divine life and Holy Spirit anointing *(2 Corinthians 3:6).* He exhibits keen spiritual discernment and divine insight into the Word of God and its personal application to believers.

• **Apostolic-Prophetic Lifestyle:** These are the people who live their lives according to the logos and rhema Word of God. The *logos* is their general standard for living and the rhema gives direction in specific areas of their lives. The fruit of the Holy Spirit is their characteristic motivation, and the gifts of the Spirit are their manifestation to meet the needs of mankind.

They are allowing their lives to become a prophetic expression of Galatians 2:20 *(KJV); 'I am crucified with Christ; nevertheless I live; yet not I, but Christ liveth in me: and the life which I now live in the flesh I live by the faith of the Son of God, who loved me, and gave Himself for me,'" (p279-281 & 289).*

The apostolic is in full swing. The best is yet to come. Much is being restored back to the church and we will see the power of the early church. The days of "Ananias and Sapphira" will return - where the fear of God will reign again and those outside the church walls will respect her position of authority on the earth.

There is power and authority when the apostolic ministry is allowed to function and flow by the Spirit of

God, just as they were supposed to. I look forward with great expectation and anticipation to the complete restoration of all such things.

CHAPTER 7

Relationship between the Apostolic and the Local Church

Let's look at the relationship that should exist between the apostle and the local church - how they should relate. We will look at how the authoritative structure within the church works. Also we will look at gifts - for example is an apostle a position of "office" or a "gift?" This we can answer straight away:

First the apostle was given as a gift, as seen in Ephesians 4:11-; 1 Corinthians 12:28. God has appointed ministry gifts in the church and this guarantees that they *(the church)* will function properly.

Ulf Ekman explains it like this: "When the Bible says that God has appointed 'first apostles,' it does not mean that He has placed them up on a pedestral. Instead, it means that the apostle has been placed *at the very front*. The idea of a vertical triangle with some sort of pope seated at the top should be discarded. Imagine instead a horizontal triangle that looks like a plow. God has positioned the apostle at the tip of this plow. The apostle can be likened to a *general practitioner*. He has the ability to operate in all of the ministry offices" (*"The Prophetic Ministry,"* p35).

"Apostle and prophet teams then set pastors and pastoral elders over the churches to guard, feed and lead the flock of believers like a shepherd *(Acts 15:32; 16:4,18,25; 2 Corinthians 1:19; 2 Thessalonians 1:1; Acts 20:28)*" (*"Apostles, Prophets and the Coming Moves of God,"* p53).

In other words the apostle has a governing office and can function in any of the gifts. Therefore the apostle has an office to govern, along with ministry gifts and the authority to establish.

Not all apostles travel, some are senior pastors of apostolic churches; apostle James is an example, he was considered an apostle in scripture, he did not actually leave the church in Jerusalem. Seemingly, he never ministered outside of Jerusalem. But apostle Paul travelled continually during his thirty-plus years of ministry.

His longest stay at any local church was two years in Ephesus. So this begs the question; **"can an apostle be a 'sent-one' and be a 'stayed-one' at the same time?"** Yes! So long as he is *establishing, building* and *fulfilling* a mandate that he has ultimately been sent by God to fulfil.

However this depends largely on his "gifting" too and not just his "office." Now his *office* is one thing, and his *gifting* helps him to carry out the mandate upon his *office*. For example, an apostle whose main gifting is to be a pastor, is able to *build* right where he is. He is able to have an international mind-set *(not parochial in his vision)* and possess the spiritual capacity to travel and be "sent" but also has the capacity to "stay."

Now in addition to this, it must be stated that all the gifts are EQUAL - they just have different tasks to do. Likewise all the "offices" are *equal;* they just operate with different gifting. For example a local elder who has a governing-office to "oversee," is one who has been given dominion in a certain area.

However when it comes to the local church in relation to the apostle - it has to be said that being part of one Body - includes being **"connected"** with the rest of the Body. And a great part of what the apostle does is through "connections." **He is a great connector.** The Holy Spirit uses the apostolic ministry more than any other to do His great global networking!

Now having said all this - any position of authority or given office of governing authority *(whether apostle, elder/ bishop)* is not dictatorial but submissive - particularly the apostle who is able to "recognise" what God has already established and continues to establish.

It is also crucial to observe here that once the local elders have been set in and their role established - it is THEY who have the authority over the local church and *not* the apostle.

Now of cause he still has authority to bring correction like a shepherd-father-figure would - but he does not stay around to carry this out. His role is to oversee.

To view this in scripture we go to the verses quoted below in order to highlight or showcase this point perfectly - when Paul was troubled to write with much concern to warn the church in Corinth of his pending rebuke!

> *I'm afraid that I may come and find you different from what I want you to be, and that you may find me different from what you want me to be... I already warned you when I was with you the second time, and even though I'm not there now, I'm warning you again. When I visit you again, I won't spare you. That goes for all those who formerly led sinful lives as well as for all the others. Since you want proof that Christ is speaking through me, that's what you'll get. Christ isn't weak in dealing with you. Instead, he makes his power felt among you. He was weak when he was crucified, but by God's power he lives.*
> *(2 Corinthians 12:20; 13:3-4 GW)*

Obviously the apostle has a continuing position of responsibility when it comes to the local church but he is not there to stay and to "RUN" the local church or implement the local vision! This again is the role of the set leading elders.

Let us move on now to the next step and take a look at how apostolic teams in particular should function and work together. Before we do this let me point out ever so briefly how important structure is. The spine or backbone is our natural structure. None of us can live without it! And spiritually speaking the same is true also. Even Satan's kingdom has structure to it.

We see this show-cased in the sixth chapter of the book of Ephesians and verse 12 where it says; "This is not a wrestling match against a human opponent. We are wrestling with rulers, authorities, the powers who govern this world of darkness, and spiritual forces that control evil in the heavenly world" *(GW)*. It is very distinct here that there are varying levels in the kingdom of darkness, levels of authority or hierarchy to execute its mandates.

This represents none other than a governing "structure," yet perhaps in reverse from that of the Kingdom of God. And by saying, **in reverse** I don't suggest for a moment that this means *equal-to* God's Kingdom, by no means! Yet Satan once knew just how the Kingdom of God functioned and was internally structured… therefore he most certainly would have modelled his best attempts at organizing his hordes of darkness - upon what he saw working with pristine order and condition within the Kingdom of God!

Structure is valued by those who understand how it works and by structure I don't mean that we get all wrapped up in knots because we have adopted some form of legalism, nevertheless "structure-less-ness" is far from freedom - but more like anarchy and chaos and who can have success in the midst of confusion?

Anyhow take business for example; they could never thrive without structure. Organizations would collapse the world over without structure and so would every great building of antiquity that we know! From the tower of London and Big Ben to the Eiffel tower - still known as the tallest structure in Paris! Nothing of significance can remain standing without some form of structure holding it up!

So **we must not be "structure-shy" especially within the church** where we tend to feel obliged to run a "free-for-all" and expect it to work! **It must not be said by our enemies that the Body of Christ has no backbone or that we are spineless!** But nor let us try and create our own image of structure based upon what we think church should be like... No! Rather we should submit ourselves to what God has already laid out in scripture to work irrespective and notwithstanding our misguided reservations towards... the apostolic ministry!

Instead we should shout, "Welcome back!" For the church as we know it - has indeed been feeble and without strength - yes even much of it has been guilty of being spineless and void of spiritual backbone! But now is the time to embrace true spiritual structure as Christ deemed fit to bestow upon the church and to recognize once again the importance of this "apostolic ministry" within His Body. Who are we to resist any rate? We must work-with and not against true spiritual structure.

It is true to say that it has never been enough for the spiritually immature - "floppy-n-floaty" (*freshly filled with new wine Christians*) to get this great and awesome job done! Nor has it ever been enough just for the "stuffy-n-religious-bookworm-types" to give their official nod to everything!

What we need is the precious working of God's Holy Spirit, the power of His Word and the coming together of His mighty Body worldwide - "a-great-working-together" - to get this great and divine commission complete!

So as we continue then, from our brief look at the supposed "hierarchy" of Satan's kingdom - let's us now look at the "structure-of-authority" as it should exist within God's Kingdom - according to scripture *(in other words apostolic teams working together)* - as follows:

1). Main Forces of Human Leadership:

A] Apostolic teams and Presbyteries *(elders):*

1. Both usually PLURAL.
2. A shepherd is a pastor.
   a) Shepherd *(singular)* always refers to Jesus *(Acts 20:17).*
   b) Elders *(plural)* are overseers *(or bishops)* or shepherds *(see also 1 Peter 5:1-2).*
3. As shepherds *(elders)* are united, so will their flocks be.

B] Elder's Responsibility is to Govern - Conservation *(1 Timothy 5:17; Titus 1:5):*

   a) In the O.T. the elder's place was at the gate.
   b) Their function: judgement, counsel and government.
   c) The N.T. concurs with this.

C] Apostolic Team's Function is Extensive *(Romans 15:20-21)*:

    a) Reach the unreached.

    b) They did not operate alone.

D] Governing Body in an Area is Sovereign:

    a) Same applies to a family, mother and father are sovereign.

    Independence and sovereignty are not the same.

    b) Sovereign: accountable to God.

    c) Independent: out from under God's authority possibly?

E] Apostolic Teams:

    Mobile

    Top Authority of Church Extension

    Presbyteries

    Local/Resident

    Govern Locally Conservation

    a) Balance is 50% emphasis on either side in N.T church.

    b) The current balance is 98% conservation and 2% extension.

F] There is *no Place for Independence* in Christianity:

2). Interdependence:

A] Apostles Appoint Elders *(Acts 14:21-23)*:

    a) After elders become installed, a group of believers becomes a church.

B] Apostles sent out by Elders *(Acts 13:1-4):*

  a) They became apostles after being prayed for and sent out *(Acts 14:14).*

  b) They were selected by the Holy Spirit from the most experienced and fruitful.

  c) Then new leadership emerges from the less experienced.

C] Reproductive Cycle *(Acts 16:1; 1 Thessalonians 2:6):*

  a) Apostle means; one sent forth.

  b) It all starts with God the Father.

3). Jesus Set the Pattern:

A] The first Apostle *(Hebrew 3:1):*

  a) Women have a place *(Luke 8:1-3).*

B] The Early Church was mobile:

C] Apostolic Attestation:

  a) It takes the supernatural to make Gentiles obedient *(Romans 15:18-19).*

  b) *(2 Corinthians 12:12)*

D] Marks of the Apostle:

  a) Perseverance, character, not giving up.

  b) Signs, wonders and mighty deeds.

E] The issue is NOT Apostle Succession, but Apostolic Ministry *(1 Corinthians 4:20):*

❖

CHAPTER 8

Honouring your Apostle

Leaders themselves must be responsible to Tithe the Tithe! "Give these instructions to the Levites: When you receive from the people of Israel the tithes I have assigned as your allotment, **give a tenth of the tithes you receive -A TITHE OF THE TITHE- to the LORD...**

You must present one-tenth of the tithe received from the Israelites as a sacred offering to the LORD. This is the LORD's sacred portion, and you must present it to Aaron the priest. **Be sure to give to the LORD the best portions of the gifts given to you"** *(Numbers 18:26-29 NLT)*.

Out of interest the same scripture in the Message Bible reads: "When you get the tithe from the people... **you must tithe that tithe and present it as an offering to GOD. Your**

offerings will be treated the same as other people's gifts... This is your procedure for making offerings to GOD **from all the tithes you get from the People... give GOD's portion from these tithes to Aaron the priest. Make sure that GOD's portion is the best... and holiest of everything you get"** *(Numbers 18:26-29).*

One of the questions that I had for many years regarding finance was in relation to *"Does a leader need to tithe the tithe?"* The answer to this is found right here in Numbers 18:26-29 where the Levite priests were commanded to pay a tithe from the tithe that they received from the people and give it to Aaron. We can call this, **"The Aaron's Tithe."**

And we see very clearly that the priests lived off of the tithe, something that we must be clear about in our teaching when we teach on the subject of *God's ways of Financial Increase.* Then in regard to church leadership, pastors and directors of Christian organizations or apostolic networks, the principle remains the same; that if we teach one thing and then excuse ourselves because of our preference of position - this is completely hypocritical.

Many pastors of churches give offerings *(but they don't necessarily tithe)* - like for example towards the random itinerant ministry gifts that come through and ministers in their churches, including towards their own structural developments and outreach projects.

Now of course these things are wonderful but it is not what God was instructing in Numbers 18:26-29; and such *gifts* are geared to sure up one's own agenda rather than giving the best and holiest to God, which is what tithing for leaders on this level is all about.

Now developing the Vision that God has given us is not wrong in itself, nor is it wrong encouraging our members to give into certain projects that in turn will enhance them. And yes teaching our people to tithe and give offerings into the storehouse so that there is meat in God's house and an open heaven where they can prosper is all good. On the other hand however when you step back and look at this theory, superficially it all looks wonderful when actually it is also teetering over the trap of deception.

For instance I believe that in these end times not only will there be a greater development of networking, where ministries are concerned, but also the network of spiritual fathering via the Apostolic Ministry. It's important to remain connected, committed and under the right structural covering. For example every leader or pastor needs to be in a relationship that is accountable in an apostolic way.

Even as an apostolic itinerant ministry myself, I can say that my wife and I are committed to other leaders that God has directed us to be accountable to, including our own pastor who is our apostolic covering. And this carries the point over that not only are our individual members called to be responsible through their connection with their local church and with their leadership, but we as ministers also must experience connectedness with the wider Body and specifically apostolically, because essentially the life flow of God's anointing and blessing comes so richly and through these avenues of: connectedness, apostolic relationship and unity *(Psalm 133:1, 3).*

And while it's important to teach our lay people all about tithing we also, as organizational leaders, ministries and churches also ought to be tithing faithfully to God through "tithing the tithe" to those whom God has specifically connected us to apostolically speaking. As leaders we are not "exempt" from tithing, rather we should be "exemplary" in it by giving tithe to the "Aaron" that God has specifically placed in our lives.

So... this is where we place the tithe of the tithe - not to random itinerant ministries or events *(that flow in and out of our lives without accountability)*. When we tithe in a correct manner, we are tithing the best of the best "unto the Lord." And to this you might say, "well I'm connected and in relationship with so many!" While this might be correct, ask yourself, of all those you are "connected" to **who is your pastor or apostle?**

Who has been assigned to be an Aaron in your life? This is something that has to be settled between you and God and not something you can change or rearrange, *(like the goal posts)* when it suits you!? Again the question has to be asked, "who do you ultimately submit to besides the Lord? And who represents God in your life? Who can speak for Him when you are not seeing straight?"

We are discussing a certain figure in your life who goes beyond mere acquaintance or friendship; someone who has a "voice" into your life, a voice that holds considerable "weight" when it really matters? Whoever that person is, then this is where you should be tithing your tithe *(the best and holiest part of everything given to you...v29)* to honour the Lord. And I don't mean your wage; I mean 10% of the income of the WHOLE of your ministry or church. Re-read Numbers where it says "the best of everything."

I stress this is not an idea of mine that I have stumbled across, nor is it an effort to conjured up finances for my own ministry! As much as I relish the support that we so need, **I am rather forced to correct an "incorrectness" that exists in the Body by addressing this subject and using very clear scriptural instruction to do so, that is very often swept under a religious and proverbial carpet!** *(We often conveniently sidestep such issues especially those that threaten our personal economy and create a levy upon our finances!?)*

But if we will obey scripture on this point, then this will not only release an open heaven over our personal lives as ministers but will flow down through every branch of our Vision *(it is our tithe that opens up the floodgate.)* And then of course our offerings that go to those random itinerant ministries on occasion, can still bring a harvest of supply to our ministries and churches that will positively affect all of our people and only then will we be living what we teach.

Let me say, that during my travels over many years, I discovered that many pastors possess the attitude, that their own ministries are the only ones within the church that should receive a *wage* or the tithe of the tithe. However let me ask, *"IS THIS GOD'S WAY?"* I don't believe it is.

Simply because now we have various *gifts* starting churches - just to *finance* their ministries! They play the role of a pastor, with the notion that this is the only way to fund their true ministry identity. People have hidden behind the safe title of "pastor" for generations, because it is unassuming and less offensive. Nevertheless it is unscriptural for *everyone* to relinquish their true identities and callings within the Body, in order to become pastors.

It's ludicrous and only with a restoration of all-things-apostolic can these haphazard notions be lifted. It has caused internal restrictions within the Body of Christ, not allowing gifts to function as they truly should and as God designed to best benefit the whole church.

Clearly then what is really needed is a return towards the apostolic and apostolic teams working together within the Body, where all gifts are recognized and can enhance one another to create a balanced fivefold ministry for its people. With a financial structure capable of supporting it with regular income and causing each *gift* to thrive and not just *survive* in the wrong position.

God has made every provision for us to be successful and to remain so. My ministry motto has always been; **"His voice is all the provision you need."** Because every instruction we need is right within His Word. If we fall short, it is only when we negate on that Word or fail to obey it..!

❖

CHAPTER 9

Establishing Leadership

I t is my desire in this chapter to help people understand whether they are *called or appointed* by God, to whatever position or realm He has decided. We are not looking here to discover the depths of how a ministry operates in its function, but simply how to be prepared in the positioning of ourselves within the Body of Christ. Only then will those in authority be able to **recognise** that which God has imparted within us; which in turn *releases* us into our destiny.

The democratic society we live in is far removed from the definition of a kingdom, where a king rules because he inherited the throne! Democracy differs in that her leaders are elected and not inherited. A system where leadership roles are open to the talented and asserted, but as for the Kingdom of God, it operates on an entirely different premise.

...I warn everyone among you not to estimate and think of himself more highly than he ought [not to have an exaggerated opinion of his own importance], but to rate his ability with sober judgment, each according to the degree of faith apportioned by God to him.
(Romans 12:3 AMP)

Jesus himself appointed offices of service, found in Ephesians 4:11, only Jesus Himself through the Holy Spirit gives this authority to men. **When we assume authority rather than receive authority we are on dangerous ground.** Self-exaltation, is the promotion of self-purposes rather than seeking first the Kingdom of God. Consider those who have been called but not yet appointed, who then commission themselves and who end up serving themselves; our commission can only come from the Lord.

Spiritual leaders are **"...chosen from among men"** and are **"...appointed** to act on behalf of men in things relating to God." Furthermore, **"one does not appropriate for himself the honour... but he is called by God..."** Just as Jesus, "...did not exalt Himself...but was **appointed..."** *(Hebrews 5:1,4,5 AMP)*

Appointment comes from God alone, even Jesus did not assume His place, but was appointed by the Father. We may be called, but we also require appointment. Consider Paul who in Romans 1:1 in the NIV states that he was both *"called"* and *"separated."*

The call comes first then the appointment! You may have been called before the earth began or while you were still in the womb but that was not when you stepped into your **"office!"** You step into your call *[salvation]* before you ever step into your office.

Note: Paul went through years of testing once he submitted himself to the leaders at Antioch. *"They must first be tested; and then... let them serve..." (1 Timothy 3:10)*

Separated actually means chosen, Jesus said *"Many are called, but few are chosen..." (Matthew 22:14)* **Meaning that not many make it through those** *testing* **periods,** but the few who make it are those who have been successfully *separated* unto the Lord! All ministries must go through a period of testing and preparation *(this preparation varies from gift to gift)* before we go through or move through into our assigned assignment, our appointed time!

There are *offices* and *positions of service,* mentioned in the bible, *(1 Corinthians 12:28)* **"And God has appointed** these in the church: first apostles, second prophets, third teachers, after that ... helps..." *(NKJ)* Paul during those first years in Antioch did not occupy a fivefold office *(Ephesians 4:11)* **in fact he served in the ministry of helps, then was promoted to the office of a teacher (2 Timothy 1:11; Acts 13:1).**

John Bevere says in his book, "Not only would Paul be tested in the realm of helps but in the office of teacher as well. When Paul was promoted from teacher to apostle we again see how God chooses and separates those that He wants to fill certain offices or positions" *("Thus saith the Lord," p120).*

In Acts 13:1-2 we can see how Paul is listed along with other teachers in Antioch and how the Holy Spirit wanted them to be separated unto Him. The appointed time had finally come, the one who had been called to be an apostle all those years earlier on the road to Damascus in Acts 9:15 had finally, after many years of testing and loyal service now been separated unto God to be an apostle. First he was *called* then he served in *helps,* later in the *office of a teacher* and then lastly in that of an *apostle.* Why? Because Paul was faithful, to promote the Lord and not himself *(1 Corinthians 4:2).*

Note: God used the established leadership whom Paul had faithfully served...

> *Then, having fasted and prayed, and laid hands on them,* ***THEY SENT THEM*** *away. So, being sent out by the Holy Spirit, they went...*
>
> *(Acts 13:3-4 NKJ)*

God did not use anyone Paul was not already in submission to; instead he used an established authority that had already been set up in Antioch. **God will not undermine the leadership in the Body of Christ in order to raise someone up into a position of leadership. Why, because your character is far more important than your *gifting.***

CHAPTER 10

Discernment of Gifting

L et us continue and move on and look at the concept of **"gift discernment."** Exactly what has God graced our lives with? Just like Paul, we must be able to "recognise" who we are in Christ and what we have been called to "do," without this, it is inevitable that we will both be "unfruitful" and "ineffective" - *(regardless of any good intentions!)*

Therefore we must discover what God's plan for our individual lives really is and more importantly what His plan is to benefit other people's lives through ours? Gifting is "always" for others and not for self! So along with the gift we must also recognise who is going to "benefit" and what exactly is He looking to "influence" with His Kingdom? God always has a strategy plan!

*Before I formed you in the womb I knew you, before you were born **I set you apart; I appointed you** as a prophet to the nations.*

(Jeremiah 1:5)

Evidently it becomes a major necessity for us to have clarity on this issue. We must begin by accepting the fact that "divine distinction" does exist and that we must work together with it not against it. Quite simply, there are many folks today who are failing to see this "divine distinction" not only in their own lives but also in the lives of others; as a result many are "struggling" and "straining" themselves to be something that God has not called them to be. We often succumb to the peer pressure of becoming what others perceive for us rather than what God has "appointed" for us.

Today it would be true to say that there exists so much confusion between **"Body gifting"** and **"ministry calling,"** something that has caused pain, heartache and much "disillusionment." **To help clear this up let's look at four major factors that need to be considered when it comes to ministry gifting:**

1). The Sense of Call: Today I believe that we often mix up "desire" with "call." Of course, the scripture tells us to "desire" the best gifts *(see 1 Corinthians 12:31)*. However "desire" can never override "call." First and foremost any "desires" must line up with the will of God for our lives.

2). The Desire for the Work: The call always comes first from God's point of view as we see here in Jeremiah 1:5 - "Before you were formed in the womb I called you" *(appointed, sanctified, set apart, separated, consecrated and dedicated!)* However this was news to Jeremiah! Who was less than ecstatic about the proposal! Rather he went into an immediate verbal inventory of all the excuses and reasons why the opposite was in fact true! Not unlike the rest of us do! Inadequacy often rears its ugly head in the face of stepping up to the call. Nevertheless in the midst of trauma we can discover the "desire" to serve the Lord.

With all this in mind we need to distinguish what "desire" in this context actually means. It goes beyond just a human sense of looking to "enjoy" something. Rather in this context it is more of an "inner yearning," a "knowing" that we must "face" this call or we are going to die! *(It can feel this intense; like your whole life depends on it, even before you really understand why).*

And while it might be possible to "enjoy" serving God, desire from the inner man is something quite different; that inward yearning we spoke of, goes much deeper; according to the Strong's it is akin to "jealousy" or being "zealous" *(see Greek #2206).*

3). Exercise the Gift: A man's ministry makes room for itself. A genuine call from God will manifest itself - if it is exercised properly. God does not appoint us to a position of "spiritual inertia" *(inactivity, lethargy, disinterest, inaction or unwillingness).* Rather He appoints and anoints for ACTION *(faith without works is dead!)* So there is a built-in dynamic to this "call" of God that we all face and it only finds **expression** through continual "practice" and not "theory!"

4). Fruitfulness: So many people lay claim to ministries in advance of "fruitfulness" and "appointment," when in fact fruitfulness is the real sign of ministry. **"Do not neglect your gift,** which was given you through a prophetic message when the body of elders laid their hands on you" *(1 Timothy 4:14);* **"fan into flame the gift** of God," *(2 Timothy 1:6);* "Each one should **use whatever gift** he has received to serve others, faithfully administering God's grace in its various forms" *(1 Peter 4:10).*

There is a distinction in kind, between a talent, which we were born with and a gift imparted by the Holy Spirit. It is noticeable in Paul's ministry that he was not averse to using his natural talents in his service for the Lord. For example he was obviously intellectually gifted but also practically so and at times used his natural abilities to support his own ministry *(see Acts 18:3 for tent making).*

But it is also important to see how Paul laid such talents aside when it came to operating in revelation *(see 1 Corinthians 2:1-3).* God uses both in the leader but in fact, it is dedication of all that we have and are which removes the clear distinction between natural talent and divine gift in the leader.

Every Called Person has a Handicap: The great heroes of the bible had handicaps even those with mighty signs and wonders; they were mere humans with many limitations and flaws. Moses committed murder and had a terrible speech impediment. Miriam fuelled a conspiracy against Moses during the wilderness journey of the Israelites. David committed adultery and murder. A harmless little old lady intimidated Elijah. And when the chips were down, Peter denied even knowing Jesus! Saul of Tarsus rounded up Christians and threw them in jail or had them stoned and it goes on.

I like the fact that none of these heroes were larger than life on their own. It gives us hope, because most of us were anything but a success before we met the Lord. If anything, God specialises in taking people who are self-willed, arrogant, or just plain ordinary, and making a success of them. By successful, I don't mean rich and famous, but humble, loving, and generous and becoming the best they can be in Christ.

What seems to be our tragedy becomes our triumph. We learn how to turn the "messes" of our lives into "messages" and how to change the "tests" into "testimonies," and as my wife often says turn our "cares" into "prayers;" our "worry" into "worship" and last but not least how to find "peace" in the "pain." Our strength is always in God.

What is our biggest hindrance to success - is it failure? - No! We are our own hindrance! Making mistakes is not a hindrance for victory! We see in scripture when Elijah went straight from a great victory into a great flop! Jonah: everything God told him to do - he did the exact opposite! We have all come to that place where we have found our "problems" were not really the issue; instead we discovered that our "problems" were actually God given "opportunities!"

This transpires simply because problems can help make us people who reach out "past" and "beyond" our natural abilities. Whereas a person who reaches out to God without any problems or challenges whatsoever, sees little if any change, growth or increase etc.

In reality who needs to look for problems? Problems exist and God has called every one of us to be problem solvers. **Problems represent NEEDS!** Problems are not wrong. They are not negatives if we look at them positively. They are needs that God has called us and given us the ability and anointing to meet and solve. For sake of illustration there were two salesmen who came back from Africa, one was down and the other was up - thrilled to bits. One said, *"They don't wear shoes in Africa - it's hopeless."* The other said, *"No one has shoes in Africa, they all need our shoes!"*

God told us that we are to get a harvest, to multiply and reproduce. That means we must see and experience "increase" because **God has said. In other words, blessing is not a "feeling" but a "condition"** therefore it is important to consider this vital fact: God's expression for our lives is an expression of His promises.

❖

CHAPTER 11

Spiritual Gifts vs. Governing Authority

It is true to say, that being "gifted" does not automatically make you "autonomous" *(independent)*. In other words, none of us are an end in ourselves nor can we have authority in ourselves! None of us can function independently from the rest of the "Body" and thrive or survive!

In actual fact our gift only operates and functions in its fullest degree and glory when it is functioning with the rest of the Body and "submitted-to-the-correct-authorities" within the Body.

Has the Lord indeed spoken only by Moses? Has He not spoken also by us?

(Numbers 12:2 AMP)

There is some confusion at large in the Body of Christ today, over this very issue, because immaturity and misunderstanding say that because a person operates in a "gifting" *(albeit genuine)* this automatically gives him or her "governing-authority." Absolutely Not!

Let's look at it like this: it is a grave mistake to confuse mere "spiritual-gifting" with "governing-office." All of us as believers have a measure of authority but this amounts to the general believer's authority and does not include governing-authority or being in an office of authority within the Body.

Therefore having a "gift" does not give anyone of us an automatic "position-of-authority," just a general authority, which is the right of "every" believer. In fact we all have been given "significant-authority" in order to lay hands on the sick and to raise the dead!

Along with general authority as a believer we have general gifts that have been distributed amongst us - but none of this gives us an automatic "office-of-authority." To help explain this further, scripture tells us clearly that it is the Holy Spirit who is the giver of the gifts but that Jesus Himself is the One who places certain individuals into positions of "governing-authority" *(called offices)*.

An ordinary believer's authority is something we can gain overnight! But to have a "governing-authority" in the Body of Christ is something else altogether. Irreparable damage has been done because of the lack of adequate understanding in this very area. *(See 1 Corinthians 12:4-31 & Ephesians 4:11-12)*.

If a person begins to operate in a legitimate "gift" but after some time refuses to yield themselves over to an established authority structure, then that gifting will become distorted and perverted; warped and void of purity <u>because of its false agenda.</u> **It's far too easy for a person to become disillusioned when they have no real accountability.** Distortion develops with misuse and lack of submission to God's governing authorities.

The same person, who is gifted now, is not automatically ready to have "governing-authority" NOW! Mere "gifting" never gave any man "governing-authority," this only comes via divine appointment and preparation; being made ready through testing and faithful serving!

For illustration purposes let us refer to Miriam and Aaron who spoke against Moses in the bible *(Numbers 12:1-2)*. Whether they did this openly or privately is not made clear but nonetheless God heard their conversation and was not too happy about it.

We must consider that although both Aaron and Miriam were "genuinely-gifted" and already had some "position-of-authority," it was Moses nonetheless who was God's "governing-authority" at that time. Their "supernatural-gifting" *(whether legitimate or not)* - afforded neither of them any room whatsoever to usurp Moses "governmental-office."

This was a direct insult to God. So serious in fact was this offence before God that Miriam became leprous because of it *(Number 12:10)*. However both were forgiven and restored, nevertheless it reveals the dangers of *usurping* God-given and appointed authority. It illustrates perfectly the difference between mere *spiritual-gifting* and *governing-authority.*

It might be true to say that not all false prophets *set out* to be false, rather they *become* that way. Just like Miriam and Aaron would have become false, if they had continued using their "gifting" to try and *out-rank* their elder brother *[Moses].*

It must be understood therefore that no man or woman can "assume" the kind of authority that Moses had been given by God - certainly not on the grounds of "spiritual-gifting!" God alone "appoints" individuals to such positions and we can see just how vehemently God defends it!

We must never forget that none of us can successfully operate outside of God's "authority-structure," as our human ability to remain authentic, trustworthy, faithful, reliable, genuine, dependable or accurate - outside of His boundaries of authority - is zero! In fact to remain "true" rather than "false" within our gift capacity, we must remain continuously submitted to God given, ordained and appointed authority. No human reasoning or logic can add anything to or take away from this concept.

Conclusion: In short, we must learn *not* to hold our own opinions too highly or be threatened by the credentials of others. We must work hard to show ourselves approved and be diligent to get genuine instruction and guidance from the Holy Spirit; who will never lead us to usurp authority. For our gifts to flourish and to live peaceful lives we must not violate the boundaries of God's authoritative structure and governing authority. **We can only enjoy the true benefits of authority, whilst we cooperate with it!**

❖

CHAPTER 12

Authority - Who has It?

We all know that we have been given authority; through Jesus Christ to overcome in this life; to lay hands on the sick and to cast out demons etc. Spiritually speaking this means we reign in life and have dominion.

Nevertheless we are all part of the Body of Christ, which has a specific "structure" with leadership - called "church" and whether we perceive we are individually gifted or not - this gives no "automatic-right" for any of us to become a leader within the local church. *(Qualification for leadership - authoritative office if God appoints - takes a number of years).*

Given to me was all authority in heaven and on earth.
                                                    (Matthew 28:18 YLT)

In this chapter I would like to begin by speaking about the apostolic, the apostles in general. Which means this chapter is not a written "spot-light" based upon the believer's authority but more specifically in regard to the "5-fold-governmental-authority."

(Note: successive chapters will touch on elders and deacons including whether the title "Bishop" is just another word for "elder" currently mistaken as the "supreme-title" of the church, replacing that of the apostle!)

First and foremost, authority begins and ends with Christ but the question is; who else has authority? To help answer this we are going to look at the 5 fold ministry gifts, ordained by none other than Christ Himself and known as the "resurrection apostles." The one that we will focus on the most in this chapter is the apostle but before we continue let me make this statement; "authority and responsibility can only be given by those who have it."

Our opening scripture reveals very clearly that ALL authority - both in heaven and on the earth belongs to Christ. That is a lot of authority! And it's not a power sharing scheme either... all means all. Jesus will never **SHARE** authority power with anyone, but He does **GIVE** it to those He delegates *(chief components in this of course are the ascension or 5 fold ministry gifts)*.

Let's see this again briefly in the following verses: "All authority in heaven and on earth has been given to me" *(Matthew 28:18)*. "It was **he who gave some to be apostles, some to be prophets, some to be evangelists, and some** to be pastors and teachers, to prepare God's people for works of service, so that the Body of Christ may be built up" *(Ephesians 4:11-12).*

"Ministry Gifts" then, exist primarily for the building up and preparing of God's people for works of service. It could be said like this: principally they have "earthly" authority and receive their ordination directly from the Lord Himself, without human involvement. Such was the case with the original disciples who lived with Jesus during His "earthly" ministry.

Equally so, however, was the case with Paul who was "...one born out of due time..." *(1 Corinthians 15:8 KJV).* "The things that mark an apostle - signs, wonders and miracles - were done among you with great perseverance" *(2 Corinthians 12:12).*

Therefore it is true to say that the original New Testament apostles literally had "ultimate authority" on this earth, which was no small thing! For instance if there was a dispute regarding doctrine, then the apostles were the final adjudicators; they had the last say.

Some of the apostles by their very nature also fulfilled the offices of elder *(bishop)* and overseer. The reverse however does not necessarily apply. A person recognised as an elder is not automatically an apostle or other ministry gift to the church. The apostle is perhaps the most difficult of the five ministry gifts to explain.

Known to us then in more familiar terms as the "Fivefold Ministries" these are perhaps better called the "Five Ascension Gifts" as we already saw revealed in Ephesians 4:11 above: **"apostle, prophet, evangelist, pastor and teacher."**

Let me point out however, these are not just gifts of the Holy Spirit per se, they are "Office and Gifting" combined, an extension of Christ's headship ministry to the church. **Their primary ministry and function is to teach, train, activate and mature the saints for works of service** (*Ephesians 4:12-13*).

As one of the five and concerning the apostle in particular - the apostle is a **"foundation-laying"** ministry (*Ephesians 2:20)* that we see in the New Testament, establishing new churches (*i.e. Paul's missionary journeys)*, correcting error by establishing proper order and structure (*first epistle to the Corinthians)*, and acting as an oversight ministry that fathers other ministries (*see 1 Corinthians 4:15; 2 Corinthians 11:28)*.

The New Testament apostle has a **"revelatory-anointing"** (*Ephesians 3:5)*. Some major characteristics are great patience and manifestations of signs, wonders and miracles. However we will know more and see greater manifestations surrounding the ministry of the "apostle" during the peak of the Apostolic Movement to come.

A keynote to point out here of course is that no person ever went or ever will walk straight into an apostolic ministry! There is always a process just as we saw with Paul: "In the church at Antioch there were prophets and teachers: Barnabas, Simeon called Niger, Lucius of Cyrene, Manaen *(who had been brought up with Herod tetrarch)* and Saul" *(Acts 13:1).* Evidently Paul was recognised operating in other ministry gifting *(teacher)* before he was commissioned by the Holy Spirit and then "sent-out" as an apostle by *(his)* the leaders.

This is a good point to remember. In other words, no one is born an apostle. It takes serious preparation and maturity to walk in that office plus it is not chosen by the individual - rather it is bestowed upon them, at God's bidding - not their own. Paul was no volunteer! God had to throw him down off his high horse first and that was just to get his attention. Rather Jesus "informed" Paul of his selection; he was not "consulted!"

It is a sovereign act of God. Entirely for His choosing and while many are called - few are chosen; few can walk in such an office. Therefore "self-assigned" or "self-appointed" apostles are real glutens for punishment, as scripture clearly reveals that it is no walk in the park to be a genuine apostle! It's not a title for glory, it's an office of government; spiritually weighty and generally unpopular!

As spearheads and pioneers, they take the brunt of onslaught, while at the same time they faithfully lead others to victory! Not everyone has what it takes! Remembering that part of the calibre and proof of leadership is generally that other people naturally "follow!" It's self-explanatory then, that if no one is *following,* those claiming to be in "leadership" status are clearly just in wishful thinking! The gift will speak for itself.

Generally if an apostle walks in a room, his presence fills the room and is felt by everyone! They possess such "weight" in the spirit that rarely goes unnoticed. They become recognised quickly as well as targeted and spoken about quickly! *(A lot!)* These are the true joys of apostle-hood *(with its inherent and unrelenting passion)*. No one in their right mind would sign up for a role like this; rather the Lord Himself confers it on man simply because there are no volunteers!

However to continue, the apostle will usually have one or more of the other five-fold ministry gifts - as his major gifting as well; this is called his "gift-mixture." For example apostle Paul was a *teacher*. Apostle Peter was a *pastor*. Apostle Barnabas was a *prophet*. We need to look at scripture to see what kind of men these were and what they did to discover their ministries as true apostles of Christ.

> *The most important is shown in the listing found here: "Now you are the body of Christ, and each one of you is a part of it. And in the church God has appointed first of all apostles, second prophets, third teachers, then workers of miracles, also those having gifts of healing, those able to help others, those with gifts of administration, and those speaking in different kinds of tongues."*
>
> *(1 Corinthians 12:27-28)*

So does this "apostolic ministry" merely exist to "bless" or to "build?" To bless is one thing, to build is quite another. We could say it like this: to "bless" and just "excite" people all the time, requires humanism, stamina and lots of charisma! This usually results in human appreciation, generally large love-gifts and popular return bookings *(invited back!)* Yet for God this will *never* be enough! A true apostle cannot be bought or sold. He is not a crowd pleaser. Even if he does please the crowd, that's not his primary intention.

Why? Because Jesus is not just interested in *exciting crowds* but in building His church. However building with the **"Master Builder"** *(Jesus)* is genuinely **"hard work!"** It takes dedication on an unprecedented scale and life-long commitment *(the apostolic ministry is not for the faint hearted!)*

We can say it like this: all apostles are in it for the long haul. They don't need convincing. They don't even "sprint!" Rather they plod, even when everyone else is having a spiritual sugar rush; running here and there on nervous human energy! In fact by the time others collapse from weariness, the apostle just keeps on keeping on, steady and undeterred. Mature with lengthy "staying-power" - because he has had to learn to "suffer-LONG!"

Apostles generally show no interest for time wasting activities and are notoriously "stable." They bring order and Godly discipline wherever they go and exude an admirable "stature." People are drawn to them, for all sorts of reasons, both good and bad. In other words they can attract trouble like bees to honey, or moth to a flame simply because they have been dispatched as God's "voice" in the earth; anything and everything wants to shut them up!

In order to "build" a master plan is required and the master designer is not haphazard. The builders need insight into God's plan and strategy for the church. The apostle in close collaboration with his prophetic teammates **seeks**

always to build according to the patterns shown on the "mountain" of revelation. "They serve at a sanctuary that is a copy and shadow of what is in heaven. This is why Moses was warned when he was about to build the tabernacle: 'See to it that you make everything according to the pattern shown you on the mountain'" *(Hebrews 8:5).*

As it was in Nehemiah's day, there must be a "clearing-away" of accumulated *rubbish!* Today there exists, to a very large extent; wrong thinking in regards to the actual role of the local church. Many see it as a place to attend only when needing a *blessing.* A cavalier "easy-come-easy-go" attitude prevails.

In addition there are such individuals who perceive that they can justifiably manipulate the church in order to serve their own ends *(personal-gain - financial, sexual or otherwise)* or simply fill a vast ego! Either way Christ is not usually "front-and-centre" in those types of churches!

Then there are those churches who try to embody new ideas and structures within their services and mingle it in with the "old-way." Generally this effects no real or worthwhile change, but instead **introduces "competition" into their churches - where the old now has to compete with the new!**

We see this featured in Mark 2:21-22, "No one sews a patch of un-shrunk cloth on an old garment. If he does, the new piece will pull away from the old, making the tear worse. And no one pours new wine into old wineskins. If he does, the wine will burst the skins, and both the wine and the wineskins will be ruined. No, he pours new wine into new wineskins" *(Mark 2:21-22)*.

With all intents and purposes an apostle is a prolific "builder" and will always have that desire to BUILD. He will establish new churches and/or re-establish existing ones, but his ministry will always be the same. In fact restoration and pioneering go hand in hand for the apostle - "building" or "re-building" are the same to him - it's all "building" and is precisely what he will be found doing. It is his calling card. To bring into order **"...to build and to establish"** *(see Jeremiah 1:10; 18:9; 31:28; 33:2)*.

Philip Mohabir in his book "Hands of Jesus," *(p24, 28-29)* says that; Paul sets forth in Ephesians 4 the core values and essential virtues that form the kernel from which local church life and practice flow. They are unity expressed in diversity, maturity, stability and corporeity. The ascended Lord gave apostles, prophets, evangelists, pastors and teachers to the church to build these characteristics in the very fibre of local church life.

He has given five gifts for this purpose. We cannot do it with three or even four. In His infinite wisdom, He knew we need five. God is generous but not superfluous. Any other structure, system, strategy, or man-made method will fail to produce the kind of church that Jesus wants and for which He died.

But now is the time when the Lord is restoring the apostolic and apostles to the church. Now is the time for the whole Body of Christ to experience the authority and

anointing of apostles just as it was in the book of Acts. To see the church rise to its full potential and built according to New Testament pattern, we must rise in vision and faith. To see the church become all that the Lamb died to make it, **we need another apostolic reformation.**

In these days the Lord is preparing the church, His Bride, for glory, equipping her to reap a final gigantic harvest and at the same time preparing the world for judgement. As Dr. Sam Matthews said, let us allow the Holy Spirit to orchestrate us into a worldwide penetration of the gospel. **It is time to become part of the second apostolic reformation.** As mentioned before "The vision is rushing to completion."

The five ascension gifts are not optional extras, but essential imperatives, ordained by God for the church. Their importance and role to the Body are a divine arrangement by Father, Son and Holy Spirit. We cannot fulfil the apostolic mission of the church without their active presence. If the church 2000 years ago needed them, how much more do we need them today when the days are so much more evil? Oh, how we need them!

❖

CHAPTER 13

The Office of an Elder

So let's get back to the teaching on the apostle in regard to those who are promoting the hierarchy of bishops as the top structure of the church. In order to refresh, the word bishop simply means **"elder"** as quoted from my teaching manual entitled "The Age of Apostolic Apostleship" *(p58-59)*.

> *...I saw four and twenty elders sitting, clothed in white raiment; and they had on their heads crowns of gold.*
> *(Revelations 4:4 KJV)*

The word episkopos occurs five times in the NT: once of Christ *(1 Peter 2:25)* and in four places of "bishops" or "overseers" in local churches *(Acts 20:28; Philippians 1:1; 1 Timothy 3:2, Titus 1:7)*. The verb episkopeo occurs in Hebrews 12:15 *("watching")* and *(in some NT MSS)* 1 Peter 5:2

("exercising the oversight")... A bishop then has "oversight of," he is an "overseer." 1 Peter 5:2 says, "Feed the flock of God which is among you, taking the oversight thereof" *(KJV)*. The Greek word for "oversight" is episkopeo, Strong's #1983 - to oversee, to beware, to look diligently, take the oversight. Extra words given: direction *(about the times)*, have charge of, take aim at *(spy)*, regard, consider, take heed, look at *(on)*, mark.

So to continue let's take a look at eldership now in both the New and Old Testaments.

The Office of Elder in the Old Testament: The Hebrew word for elders: *zaqen, [OT]* does not necessarily mean an old man, but does imply one of maturity and experience *(Numbers 11:16)*. They were recognised as the highest authoritative body over the people. They acted as the religious representatives of the nation *(Jeremiah 19:1; Joel 1:14; 2:16)*.

As well as handling many political matters and settling inter tribal disputes *(Joshua 22:13-33)* the town elders were a sort of municipal council, whose duties included acting as judges in apprehending murderers *(Deuteronomy 19:12)*, conducting inquests *(Deuteronomy 21:2)* and settling matrimonial disputes *(Deuteronomy 22:15; 25:7)*.

The ***"elders of Israel,"*** first heard of in Exodus 3:16-18, were assembled by Moses to receive God's announcement of the liberation of Egypt. The covenant was ratified at Mount Sinai in the presence of 70 elders of Israel *(Exodus 24:1,9,14 cf. 19:7)*, the ***"nobles"*** *(KJV)* or chief men of the nation *(24:11)*. Later 70 elders were specially anointed with the Spirit to aid Moses in governing the nation *(Numbers 11:16-25)*. In cases when the whole community sinned, the elders of the congregation or community were to represent it in making atonement *(Leviticus 4:13-15)*.

The authority of the elders was in principle greater than that of the King *(cf, 2 Kings 23:1)*. It was this group, which demanded that Samuel appoint a king *(1 Samuel 8:4-6)*, and they were parties to the royal covenant which established David as king *(2 Samuel 5:3)*.

In Babylon the elders were the focal point of the Jewish community in exile *(Jeremiah 29:1; Ezra 8:1; 14:1; 20:1-5)*, and after the return to Jerusalem they continued active *(Ezra 5:5, 9; 6:7-8, 14; 10:8, 14)*. While their authority was originally civil, *by New Testament times* the "elders of the people" *(presbyeroi tou laou)* shared with the chief priests the power of determining religious affairs and if necessary of expulsion from the synagogue.

Elders in the New Testament: An elder in the NT is really a bishop. In his vision of heaven, John saw 24 elders seated upon thrones surrounding the throne of God, clothed in white garments and wearing golden crowns *(Revelations 4:4)*. They fall down in worship and cast their crowns before God's throne *(4:10; cf. 11:16; 19:4)*, and with their harps and bowls of incense, symbolising the prayers of the saints, they sing a new song to the Lamb *(5:8-10)*.

As elders they represent God's people; their thrones and crowns symbolise a kingly role, while their acts of worship and the bowls of incense suggest a priestly function. Thus they seem to be the chief representatives of the redeemed as a Kingdom of priestly function. *(Revelations 1:6; cf. 20:6; 1 Peter 2:5, 9; Exodus 19:6).*

They used the same word for *elder* in the OT and the NT, but the content of the Christian elder's ministry has changed, for it now includes visitation of the sick *(James 5:14).*

Elders are vital components within the structure of the church, including the restoration of the apostolic. **Elders and the apostles must work together. NOT in a power struggle but in complete unison, consulting with one another - bringing stability and strength to the local church.**

However it is true to say that as we begin to see the apostles and elders working together again like in the time of the early church, we are going to begin to see an **unleashing of God's** power - restored to the church - a power that this world will NOT be able to resist or refute! **Authority and power - go hand in hand. When perfect order is restored *(concerning authority in the local church)* there will no longer be any shortage of power - in the church of the living God.**

Looking at the early church, where elders seemed to have been **responsible** for groups of house-churches, *(at that time there were no church buildings!)* Elders were appointed to make sure these groups stayed on the right track spiritually. They exercised the greatest authority of all the members and brought a sense of the Fatherhood of God to the local church, such as: faith, security, confidence and spiritual covering.

Elders were also meant to establish and maintain a family atmosphere, which enabled the flow of love between members. This enabled the Holy Spirit to move in power and enabled new converts to be *kept secure* after any evangelistic effort. This meant they had to speak with people personally and not rule by notes in the church newsletter.

Elders were "overseers" who had spiritual responsibility for local church members. It has already been stated: it was the elders and NOT the apostles - that ruled the local churches in New Testament times. Trans-local ministries such as apostles and prophets did at times bring some correction or exhortation, but the elders carried out their task of overseeing and shepherding the local church unhindered.

From within a group of elders, God typically raises up a "set-elder" - a leader of leaders. This man is often the pastor, vicar, or full-time leader within a church. The elders may be of equal standing, but it would be very unusual for them all to be equal in leadership experience, gift and ability. The man who is called to lead the elders should enable eldership meetings by **"chairing"** them - in other words **"managing"** them and keeping them on the right track.

He is often also the spokesman for the eldership as well as being the main church teacher. Remember, every church member, including the elders, needs to submit to God and to any other person God raises up into a position of authority, e.g. an apostle bringing correction from God or a prophet bringing the "Word" of God. This submission to God and each other enables any church to be coordinated by God and fruitful as it seeks to carry out His will.

The scriptures do not reveal a clear job description for elders, but they do show us something of the way eldership functioned within the early church. Studying this can assist elders today in better understanding their significant role and what it is that God desires of them.

The qualifications we see in scripture concerning those serving in eldership - reveal the sheer **calibre and quality** of such men - chosen and expected to be fit for their task! These men had to serve the church to which they were called in a Christ-like way and other members of the church needed to recognize some measure of spiritual gifting and spiritual maturity in them.

For example those recognized, as elders should: direct the affairs of the church they were entrusted with by God, i.e. they were God's stewards *(Titus 1:1f; 1 Timothy 5:17)*. The Greek word for **"overseer"** is *episkopos* and was used in the secular writings of the time to refer to a person with **administrative and judicial functions. Therefore eldership is a governmental function, which has authority,** and whose goal in the local church is to increase and maintain the rule of God; this affects each individual member, including their respective families, the church itself and the wider community.

Remember God never instituted "DEMOCRACY" as a means of governing His people. Rather He established "THEOCRACY" which means - government by God Himself. He enables His rule by raising up leadership - through whom He can rule *(principally eldership in a local church setting)*. These men therefore, must walk closely with God and wait on Him, so that they can hear His Word for the church for which they are responsible and obey His directives and take care of God's church.

They should also have a good reputation with those outside the church so that the church will be seen as a place of integrity, where non-Christians can come for help *(1 Timothy 3:5, 7)*. They also need to work hard, help the weak and remember that it is more blessed to give than receive *(Acts 20:35)*.

They must be able to teach. The Greek word used here is **didaktikos** - better translated as "apt or skilled to teach" *(1 Timothy 3:2)*. However, 1 Timothy 5:17 suggests that only *some* had the labour *(or toil)* of preaching and teaching in the local church. This probably referred to those elders whose main function was preaching and teaching and perhaps even their full-time employment; hence the following verse about the worker deserving his wages *(1 Timothy 5:18)*. All elders need to be able to teach and disciple *(even if it is just in a one-to-one counselling situation),* however only some are called to preach and teach in a corporate sense.

Elders, when they are asked, anoint with oil in the name of the Lord those who are sick. The prayer offered in faith will make the sick person well, because the Lord will raise them up... *(James 5:14-15)* They also need to be on guard and watch over themselves and the flock of which the Holy Spirit has made them overseers/elders, because savage wolves will attempt to come in and will not spare the flock *(Acts 20:28-31)*.

In closing, elders are willing shepherds of the flock, that God has placed under their care - serving as **overseers** and **examples of Christ-likeness** to their flock *(Acts 20:28; 1 Peter 5:2-3)*. Their example should be Jesus Christ who is the **shepherd and overseer** of our souls *(1 Peter 2:25; 1 John 2:6)*. Laying hands on and praying for those in their congregation, thus imparting spiritual gifts and prophecy *(1 Timothy 4:14)*. Encourage *(or exhort)* those they oversee by sound doctrine and by holding firmly to the trustworthy message as it has been taught, and refute *(or convict)* those who oppose it *(Titus 1:9)*.

Finally elders are to discern the truth of God in a given situation and guide the church for which they are responsible in the light of that truth. **The elders in Jerusalem did this with the apostles and therefore kept the church on the right path** *(Acts 15:1-31; Acts 16:4)*.

❖

CHAPTER 14

Church Government

We were discussing the significance and the role of "elders" in both the Old and New Testaments. Specifically in the New Testament we saw that there was an addition to their function which was that of "visiting the sick" *(as seen in James 5:14)*. We also saw confirmed through scripture, that elders appear to be the "chief representatives of the redeemed" and have a "…priestly function."

> *…They continued steadfastly in the apostles' doctrine and fellowship, and in breaking of bread, and in prayers.*
>
> *(Acts 2:42 KJV)*

However as we continue in light of the apostle, it was more in a *"corporate capacity"* by which he provided leadership for the primitive church; and that leadership was effective both in **mercy** *(Acts 2:42)* and in **judgement** *(Acts 5:1-11)*.

They exercised a general authority over every congregation, sending two of their number to supervise new developments in Samaria *(Acts 8:14)* and deciding with the elders on a common policy for the admission of Gentiles *(Acts 15)*. So in this degree we can see evidenced, the apostles and elders working together for the benefit of the whole.

In Acts when the pressure of work increased, they appointed seven assistants *(Acts 6:1-6)*, elected by the people and ordained by the apostles. They were to administer to the churches charity; these seven have been regarded as deacons from the time of Irenaeus onwards, but Philip, the only one whose later history is clearly known to us, became an evangelist *(Acts 21:8)* with an unrestricted mission to preach the gospel. Church officers with a distinctive name are first found in the elders of Jerusalem, who received gifts *(Acts 11:30)* and took part in Council *(Acts 15:6)*.

This office was probably copied from the elder-ship of the Jewish synagogue; the church itself called a synagogue in James 2:2 and Jewish elders, who seem to have been ordained by imposition of hands, were responsible for maintaining discipline, with power to excommunicate breakers of the law.

But Christian elder-ship, as a gospel ministry acquired added pastoral *(James 5:14; 1 Peter 5:1-3)* and preaching *(1 Timothy 1:5)*; and although the disturbances at Corinth may suggest that a more complete democracy prevailed in that congregation *(cf. 1 Corinthians 14:26)*.

THE GENERAL PATTERN OF CHURCH GOVERNMENT IN THE APOSTOLIC AGE WOULD SEEM TO BE A BOARD OF ELDERS OR PASTORS, POSSIBLY AUGMENTED BY PROPHETS AND TEACHERS, RULING EACH OF THE LOCAL CONGREGATIONS, WITH DEACONS TO HELP IN ADMINISTRATION AND WITH A GENERAL SUPERINTENDENCE OF THE ENTIRE CHURCH PROVIDED BY APOSTLES *(NOT BISHOPS!)*

The late Dr. Bob Gordon once wrote, "There are two biblical qualifications for eldership; these are distinct from others… **elders must not be novices and that they must be able to teach.** The other qualifications are a check to make sure that those proposed for eldership are living an exemplary Christian life. Those who are to oversee the church need to be good ambassadors for it, for Christ *(i.e. be models of Christlikeness)*, and for the truths they were teaching and not merely professional leaders.

Elders therefore need to be: men of prayer, true worshippers of God, men of the Word of God, men of true spiritual authority and maturity and men of mature spiritual experience and understanding. Men who are spiritually ahead of those in the church, men of vision *(which is sourced in God)*, who receive God's guidance and revelation and who are sensitive to the moving of the Holy Spirit; and men of faith, because without faith it is impossible to please God.

Elders are recognised by who they are and not what they do, and not by age or official title. They need to be men who have largely got their spiritual priorities right and their life in spiritual order.

The qualifications in the New Testament for an elder (*overseer*) are many:

1. Shepherds of God's flock that is under their care, serving as overseers - not because they must, but because they are willing, as God wants them to be (*1 Peter 5:2*)

2. **Not greedy for money nor a lover of money** (*1 Peter 5:2; 1 Timothy 3:3*)

3. Eager to serve, of ready mind or willingly (*1 Peter 5:2*)

4. Examples to their flock, not lording it over those entrusted to them (*1 Peter 5:3*)

5. The husband of but one wife (*1 Timothy 3:2; Titus 1:6*). (*Note: divorce is allowable in scripture in certain circumstances; therefore, this phrase refers to bigamy or polygamy, not divorce*)

6. A man whose children are faithful and not accused of riot or unruly (*Titus 1:6*)

7. Blameless (*Titus 1:6-7*)

8. Not overbearing (*not self-willed*) (*Titus 1:7*)

9. Not quick tempered (*not soon angry*) (*Titus 1:7*)

10. Not given to much wine (*1 Timothy 3:3: Titus 1:7*)

11. Not violent (*no striker or brawler*) (*1 Timothy 3:3; Titus 1:7*)

12. Not pursuing dishonest gain (*Titus 1:7*)

13. Hospitable (*a lover of and given to hospitality*) (*Titus 1:8; 1 Timothy 3:2*)

14. One who loves what is good *(Titus 1:8)*

15. Self-controlled *(sober) (1 Timothy 3:2)*

16. Upright *(just) (Titus 1:8)*

17. Holy *(Titus 1:8)*

18. Disciplined *(temperate) (Titus 1:8)*

19. Able to hold firmly to the trustworthy message as it has been taught, so that they can encourage others by sound doctrine and refute those who oppose it *(Titus 1:9)*

20. Above reproach *(1 Timothy 3:2)*

21. Temperate *(vigilant) (1 Timothy 3:2)*

22. Respectable *(of good behaviour) (1 Timothy 3:2)*

23. Able *(apt or skilled)* to teach *(1 Timothy 3:2)*

24. Not quarrelsome *(contentious or given to fighting) (1 Timothy 3:3)*

25. Gentle *(patient) (1 Timothy 3:3)*

26. Not covetous *(1 Timothy 3:3 AV)*

27. Able to manage their own family well and see that their children obey them with proper respect... If anyone does not know how to manage *(rule)* their own family *(house)*, how can they take care of God's church *(1 Timothy 3:4-5)*

28. Not a recent convert *(a novice)*, or they may become conceited *(puffed up with pride)* and fall under the same judgement as the devil *(1 Timothy 3:6)*

29. Of good reputation with outsiders *(have a good testimony among those who are outside)*, so that they will not fall into disgrace and into the devil's trap *(lest they fall into reproach and the snare of the devil)* *(1 Timothy 3:7)*

30. Able to work with other men in mutual submission, because they are called to work as an eldership team and not as individuals *(elders of a congregation are always mentioned in the plural)*

Important Note: A true elder will tend the sheep whether recognised or not and will not want position or self-aggrandisement, but rather will simply want to serve the flock to which God has called him. A man who starts to do this, but gives up because he was not recognised or officially appointed, proves that he is selfishly motivated. Such a man is not serving because 'he is called to the task by God' but is serving for his own gain rather than for the good of the church," *("Master Builders," p155-156)*.

❖

CHAPTER 15

Elders are Territorial

As we continue with this concept of the apostle, we have taken the last chapters along with this one to talk about the role of elders in the Body of Christ, in yester-world and in today's-world. All authority has "influence" - and all influence has a "realm of influence" over which it operates.

> *Remember your leaders who have spoken God's Word to you. Think about how their lives turned out, and imitate their faith.*
>
> *(Hebrews 13:7 GW)*

Now we are going to look at this in terms of the world territory. So let's begin by looking at what this word **"territory"** actually means. Its literal meaning is as follows: **"an area regarded as owned by the state, social group, individual or animal."**

In addition to this, another significant word that describes territory is "province," which in times-past was the basic **"unit of administration"** within the Roman Empire. Its earliest usage, was a general term that referred to the **"magistrate's sphere of administrative action."** This term signified both the **"rule"** of the governor and the **"region"** that was entrusted to his care *(the geographical sense was dominant);* and included the **"administration of justice."** Therefore when a province was given to a governor, this was for him to: control, supervise, protect and oversee. It literally became his territory - to rule and to govern - for a specific period of time.

Now when it comes to the spiritual aspect of this matter - there are such things as **"territorial spirits"** *(which are active within the heavenly realms)* but this is another teaching altogether! However as believers it is our right to exercise our authority within any given territory and we too are meant to be territorial!

We are not merely undercover agents that live invisible to the world, with alter-egos that no one knows about! We are not a secret society! Rather we ought to govern those areas or regions that God has entrusted to us as scripture speaks about - holding-claim to every place we put our feet! *(See "Territorial Spirits" by C. Peter Wagner).*

This is too general in thought, even though all believers possess authority to a degree - not all believers are called to governmental offices - such as elders and apostles for example. So we must not over generalise this issue and so now let's go beyond this and look more closely at our opening title **"Elders are Territorial."**

This statement refers to the fact that God placed elders within the church to oversee it. Their influence was not merely for the church only, but regionally and spiritually *(in the spirit realm)*. Their influence is far reaching both practically and spiritually. For instance if we go to the Old Testament, we can see that elders often acted as "magistrates" and "judges," who represented the people. Therefore it was their job to "administrate justice" within the areas allocated to them.

Even today this whole structure has NOT changed - because of time! Rather it still continues today; the only thing that has changed is that elders today have the added responsibility of visiting and praying for the sick. They do so in the power of the name of Jesus and His blood!

Elders also represent "pillars" within the church: of maturity, wholeness, purity, integrity, righteousness, doctrine and all that is true.

Every church needs Good Elders!

How then should the church respond to such elders? Well firstly there are three major things that need to be noted from scripture.

• **Firstly: Elders are worthy of double honour,** especially those whose work is preaching and teaching *(1 Timothy 5:17)*. Church members need to respect, uphold and admonish them *(1 Thessalonians 5:12-13)*. The job of an elder is not easy and the church needs to encourage those who are overseeing them and not pull them down or make their job more difficult than it needs to be. In fact, church members should obey their elders and submit to their authority, because they are men who keep watch over the church and who are accountable before God for it *(Hebrews 13:17)*. Also, if an elder is serving the church on a full-time basis, then the scriptures tell us that the worker deserves his wages *(1 Timothy 5:18)*.

• **Secondly: Church members should not entertain an accusation against an elder unless it is brought by two or three witnesses.** Elders do not need to be the subject of gossip, which only serves to undermine their credibility and authority. Members of the church should stop people who do this and stop something getting out of hand or being blown out of proportion to the truth. However, if an elder is found to be in sin, they are to be rebuked publicly, so that others may take warning *(1 Timothy 5:19-20)*.

• **Thirdly: The church members should follow the godly example set by the elders** *(Hebrews 13:7)*.

In closing, we all know that scripture tells us to "seek first the Kingdom of God." The word Kingdom also represents the **"rule and reign"** of God in scripture. But now we look at the role of elders as they use their God given positions to reign; to rule and to exercise Godly authority wherever they are placed. They actually represent the government of God within the church and must act accordingly.

All of this ties in with the role of the apostle and the apostolic age. The elders do not function under their own authority nor do the apostles. All authority given by God must work together in unity not in contest or rivalry with each other. A house divided falls. It cannot stand and until the elders can work together with the apostles in the local church as they were ordained and equipped to do so, there will always be a certain lack of authority and power.

So bring it on! Bring on the order of God. The church is in need of her power. She needs to be stifled no longer. Let truth be taught and revelation restored to the Body of Christ. As all man-made-efforts to rule and to govern, have left her barren and lacking powerful influence within society. But if she regains her position and spiritual possession - with all her dignity in tact - the world will learn once again, what it is to FEAR the authority of the living God - that exists within the local church!

• **Finally,** in closing this chapter - my son who is 16 years old this year got talking to his mother about the story in the bible of Ananias and Sapphire. They were discussing the awesome authority that the apostle s exercised in the early church. However over lunch our son came up with this honest and simple question (*and I quote him word for word simply because I think others would ask the same question!*): **"If the apostle is being 'restored' where did he go? What happened to him?"**

This legitimate question was deserving of a simple reply! "The fact of the matter is…" I told him, "the apostle never went anywhere! He is not the one being restored, rather the truth about his *role* is being restored to the Body of Christ." "Why?" "Because over time, truth was replaced by deception and distortion."

Which brings us to our closing statement. When TRUTH is fully restored to the church *(before Christ returns)* via the revealed Word of God *(the teaching of "revelation")* the apostle will be able to take his rightful place, along with the elders. No longer stuffy relics of an age-old institute or relegated to stain- glass-windows of rotting church buildings. No! They will not remain this ineffective but will take their rightful places in their intended role as POWERFUL EXECUTORS OF GOD'S AUTHORITY & JUSTICE.

The government of God within the local church is vital. The apostle has a huge part to play in this, along with the elders. **May this RESTORATION OF TRUTH advance with speed!** How the church needs her divine order - just as God planned it and not as man distorted it - by humanistic ideals and **replacement theology!**

❖

CHAPTER 16

Promoting the Lord or Self?

There are certain individuals today who assume that they are in leadership when in actual fact they have never legitimately qualified for such position; rather born from ego and hidden agenda than the high calling of God!

> *People should think of us as servants of Christ and managers who are entrusted with God's mysteries. Managers are required to be trustworthy.*
> *(1 Corinthians 4:1-2 GW)*

So how do we recognise such individuals without starting a witch-hunt!? Well they are really quite easy to spot but having said that, what is obvious to the trained eye is not necessarily obvious to the untrained and therefore spiritually vulnerable.

To begin with they are made up of the type of individuals who have for one reason or another been around the church world for many years and have a good grip on Christian "jargon" and "philosophy" yet more out of "head knowledge" and "learnt-behaviour" than of genuine "living connection" with God! They come to believe that they have in some way been automatically chosen to be a *voice* to the church!

They even suppose that they have some sort of special "supernatural qualifications!" and are convinced that they have some "special insights" that we all need - along with "special authority" to bring "correction" wherever they feel necessary - even to the entire Body at large! So we must not fail to ask them, "Who are you and who has qualified you to be in such position?" Once they open their mouths they usually reveal themselves!

To keep things positive let's look at what qualifies a leader rather than what doesn't. According to scripture, there are two major qualifications for leadership.

• **First** of all there must be fruit; fruit of lifestyle and then fruit of ministry.

• **Secondly** there must be recognition and appointment *(see Acts 5:1-11; 6:1-7; Ephesians 4:11)*. But first we must look for the fruits; it's okay having a big mouth, but where is the fruit!? Here are some scriptures concerning the "fruit of lifestyle" *(Galatians 5:22; Romans 12:3; 1 Timothy 3:1-f; Titus 1:5-16)*.

Consider our example in this matter; Paul the apostle, who went through years of "testing" once he submitted himself to the leaders at Antioch. *"They must first be tested; and then...let them serve..."* (1 Timothy 3:10) According to this particular scripture, once the "testing" part stops, the "serving" part begins! As Paul found out, this took considerable time.

It remains a fact today that in God's Kingdom the way up is always down and the greatest amongst us is the servant of all. It is only the world that glories in arrogance and "ostentatious crowd-pulling" *(entertaining never qualified anyone for leadership!)* **Someone with a servant's heart is not** *showy or flamboyant* **but humble.** This is a good sign of leadership quality. In fact, for anyone who has genuinely been called to a leadership position within the Body of Christ, one of **the first things that the Holy Spirit is going to deal with is** *...ego!*

Yet as first mentioned above, certain individuals have the ability to "learn behaviour" that seems to be humble when in actual fact it is known as "false-humility." Perhaps we have become so familiar with the false that we no longer recognise the true. True humility is *often* misinterpreted. Therefore we MUST be led by the Spirit, without Him we are spiritually dull and cannot see. We have eyes to see and yet cannot see; ears to hear but cannot hear. Only the Holy Spirit can REVEAL all truth to us and keep us spiritually alert *(John 16:13).*

He is the Father's complete provision for us - so that we cannot be so easily misled. But if we choose to walk without Him, to be vulnerable and spiritually ignorant, then no one can be blamed but ourselves! Yet we are meant to be "Over-Comers" in Christ, not gullible or easily led astray, but spiritual laziness is often the cause of dullness *(see apostasy)*.

Now let us emphasise once again the fact that all potential leaders are "separated" or "set apart" by God *(it is never a **natural** selection; as seen in 1 Samuel 16:7)* and this "separation" actually means *"chosen."* Jesus Himself said, *"Many are called, but few are chosen..."* (Matthew 22:14 KJV), meaning that not many make it through the *"testing"* part! Yet the few who do are successfully "separated" unto the Lord *(so not everyone who claims to be a leader, is one!)*

While many want the name-tag of "leadership" not many want the "costs" or "associated risks!" And while the "separating process" was never intended to be easy, according to scripture, anyone caught "shortcutting" is not legitimate! *(John 10:7; Matthew 7:13)*

Now let's recap on what we said in Chapter nine: There are "offices" and "positions of service" mentioned in the bible, *(1 Corinthians 12:28). "And God has appointed these in the church: first apostles, second prophets, third teachers, after that ... helps..." (NKJ)* Once again notice that during those first years in Antioch Paul did *not* occupy a "fivefold-office" *(see Ephesians 4:11)* but instead served in the ministry of helps, only then did he progress to the office of "teacher" *(see 2 Timothy 1:11; Acts 13:1).*

In Acts 13:1-2 we can see how Paul was listed along with other teachers in Antioch and how the Holy Spirit wanted them to be specifically "separated" unto Him. The appointed time had finally come, the one who had been called to be an apostle all those years earlier on the road to Damascus in Acts 9:15 had finally, after possibly 14 years of testing and loyal service, was successfully "separated" unto God to be an apostle. First he was **"called"** then served in **"helps,"** then he progressed to the office of a **"teacher"** and finally the office of an **"apostle."** Why? The reason: Paul was faithful to promote the Lord and not himself *(see 1 Corinthians 4:2).*

CHAPTER 17

Your Destiny is developed in Adullam

God has prepared a company of people with an anointing to breakthrough into the God-ordained destiny for their lives as well as for cities and nations. Many of these people are the most unlikely in the natural to be chosen by the Lord. How He loves to take the least likely and demonstrate His ability through them!

David was one of those "unlikely" people that God used to accomplish colossal breakthroughs. Just as the church is stepping into a new season, David came forth at a time when the Lord was transitioning His people from an old religious order *(Eli)* to a fresh new move of His Spirit *(David)*. Whenever God brings His people to a major juncture in history, He always raises up prophets to declare it.

The prophet Samuel stood at a major juncture in history and poured the anointing oil on young David. He declared a new authority was arising to defeat the powers of the enemy and release the will of God in the earth. "Then Samuel took the horn of oil and anointed him in the midst of his brothers; and the Spirit of the Lord came mightily upon David from that day forward..." *(1 Samuel 16:13 NASB)*

And such as do wickedly against the covenant shall he corrupt by flatteries: but the people that do know their God shall be strong, and do exploits.

(Daniel 11:32 KJV)

David received his **"first anointing"** in the midst of his own brothers. In an *obscure* place God chose an unlikely individual to accomplish great Kingdom exploits *(Daniel 11:32)*. Unfortunately those close to David didn't embrace such an anointing on his life!

As with David, there are people who have known you in the old season of your life. Some of them will try to hold you to an old place, familiar to them. They want you to do the same things you did in the old season. They might enjoy your company but **don't want to go where you are going.**

After David received this "first anointing," he came face to face with the giant Goliath. **The enemy loves to challenge the new anointing in your life.** He doesn't want you to move forward. However, war was not new to David. He had defeated the lion and the bear during the old season. Now he faced the enemy that was resisting David's destiny. An incredible courage rose up in David as he asked the question, "Is there not a cause?" *(1 Samuel 17:29 KJV)*

David was not in the battle for his own benefit. He realized there was a cause at stake, the advancement of God's Kingdom in the earth. Those who will be part of the Davidic Company that God is raising up in this hour must be free from fears and selfish interests. It is a time when fears must be replaced with great courage! During this time, we must deal with insecurities, intimidation, limitations, and jealous spirits. All of these are designed to keep this Davidic Company from God's destiny.

After David's "first anointing," he ended up in a dark place. "So David departed from there and escaped to the cave of Adullam; and when his brothers and all his father's household heard of it, they went down there to him" *(1 Samuel 22:1 NASB).*

Adullam was a place of darkness, obscurity and confusion. God's future generals often find themselves in obscure places. However, in the dark place of Adullam, David found a place of prayer. **As the seed of destiny dies, we learn that God is our only hope.** In the times of weakness, the Lord becomes our strength *(2 Corinthians 12:9).*

During David's hour of unpopularity, he discovered who the people were that would stand with him. Real friends are committed to you in the good and the hard times. Only those who have true heart connections will stand with you in difficult days. The Body of Christ is in a time when we will know those whose hearts are knitted to our hearts.

God gathered around David those who were discontented, and those in debt *(1 Samuel 22:2).* From a small number of unlikely people, God brought forth from the cave a powerful army of 340,000 recruits! The hidden place became a place of multiplication.

Today, God is assembling His army. God's Army is made up of those generals who have been in a hidden place in the last season. Their hearts have been knitted together to see King Jesus exalted in the earth. They have come forth with the anointing at Judah. David received his **"second anointing"** at Judah. Judah means praise. **Praise will be a key to victory.**

The seed of destiny in these lives that seemed dead is coming forth now in resurrection life and power! David received his **"third anointing"** at Hebron. Hebron was a place of alliance. It was the place of making commitments, entering relationships and cutting covenants. As a result of these alliances, David and his army was able to take back ground the enemy had stolen.

They were able to declare that God is God of the Breakthrough. "So David came to Baal-parazim and defeated them there; and he said, *'The Lord has broken through my enemies before me like the breakthrough of waters.'* Therefore he named that place Baal-perazim" *(2 Samuel 5:20 NASB).*

God is gathering a powerful group of people in these days. Lives are joining together in covenant relationships. Ministries are aligned to see the Kingdom of God advance through the earth. Many of the ministries have been in Adullam in the past season. However, they are being properly aligned so the seed of destiny in them is released to accomplish great Kingdom exploits.

Destiny has a time for fulfillment. **Great courage will be needed as we embrace our destiny.** These are days when we will see new enemies. Old war strategies and independent spirits will not be able to stand against these enemies. A synergistic alliance of powerful visionary ministries is emerging as a Davidic Army for the new season. They are anointed for powerful breakthrough in cities, territories and nations. Their testimony proclaims, *"Jesus is God of the Breakthrough!"*

Forward or Pass it On!

Note: If this book has blessed you, let it bless others. Share it, and let the message bear fruit in someone else's life. *"What you have heard... entrust to... others"* (2 Timothy 2:2). Why not sow by gifting a copy, or even placing a bundle in the hands of your home group or church? In this way the truth multiplies and glorifies our Heavenly Father.

A massive Thank You

❖

Bibliography

- Bevere, John. Thus Saith the Lord? (120) Lake Mary, Florida USA: Published by Creation House, A Division of Strang Communications Company. Copyright © 1999

- Ekman, Ulf. The Apostolic Ministry. (20-21, 23) Uppsala, Sweden: Published by Word of Life Publications. Copyright © 1995

- Ekman, Ulf. The Prophetic Ministry. (35) Uppsala, Sweden: Published by Word of Life Publications. Copyright © 1990

- Gordon, Bob, and David Fardouly. Master Builders. (155-156) Chichester, England: Published by Sovereign World. Copyright © 1990

- Hamon, Bill. Apostles, Prophets and the coming moves of God. (14, 279-281, 289) Shippensburg, Pennsylvania USA: Published by Destiny Image Publishers, Inc. Copyright © 1997

- Mohabir, Philip. Hands of Jesus. (24, 28-29) Thisted, Denmark: Published by Powerhouse Publishing. Copyright © 2003

- Pateman, Alan. The Age of Apostolic Apostleship. (58-59) Florence, Italy: Published by APMI Publications. Copyright © 2011

- Strong, James. S.T.D., L.L.D. 1890. Strong's Exhaustive Concordance; Dictionaries of the Hebrew and Greek Words. e-Sword ® version 7.6.1 Copyright © 2000-2005. All Rights Reserved. Registered trade mark of Rick Meyers. Equipping Ministries Foundation. USA www.e-sword.net.

- Unless otherwise indicated, all scriptural quotations are from the HOLY BIBLE, NEW INTERNATIONAL VERSION ®. NIV ®. Copyright © 1973, 1978, 1984 by the International Bible Society. Used by permission of Zondervan Publishing House. All rights reserved.

- Scripture quotations marked AMP are taken from The Amplified Bible. Old Testament copyright © 1965, 1987 by Zondervan Corporation, Grand Rapids, Michigan. New Testament copyright © 1958, 1987 by The Lockman Foundation, La Habra, California. All rights reserved.

- Scripture quotations marked AV are taken from the American King James Version.

- Scripture references marked BBE are taken from the Bible in Basic English Version of the Bible by Professor Samuel Henry Hooke.

- Scripture references marked GW are taken from GOD'S WORD®, © 1995 God's Word to the Nations. Used by permission of Baker Publishing Group.

- Scripture references marked KJV are taken from the King James Version of the Bible.

- Scripture references marked MSG are taken from The Message. Copyright © 1993, 1994, 1995, 1996, 2000, 2001, 2002. Used by permission of NavPress Publishing Group.

- Scripture references marked NASB are taken from the NEW AMERICAN STANDARD BIBLE®, Copyright © 1960,1962, 1963, 1968, 1971, 1972, 1973, 1975, 1977, 1995 by The Lockman Foundation. Used by permission.

Bibliography

Drs Alan and Jennifer Pateman

Senior and Co-Apostles

Drs Alan and Jennifer Pateman, missionaries
from the UK, who at present reside in Tuscany, Italy,
and travel together as an apostolic couple. They
are the Founders of Alan Pateman World Missions,
Connecting for Excellence International,
and LifeStyle International Christian University.
President and Vice President of
World Missions Ministries Association
and APMI Publishing/Publications.

*(Please see our website for all profile and
international information, itinerant, conferences
and graduations, etc.)*

www.AlanPatemanWorldMissions.com

❖

To Contact the Author

Please email:

Alan Pateman World Missions

Email: apostledr@alanpatemanworldmissions.com
Web: www.AlanPatemanWorldMissions.com

*Please include your prayer requests
and comments when you write.*

❖

Other Books

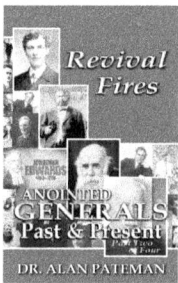

Revival Fires - Anointed Generals
Past & Present (Part Two of Four)

Seasons might be changing but God's Word remains the same. The heart of the author is to help train, equip and be a blessing to those men and women who will be willing to fulfil their potential in ministry and be properly equipped for service.

ISBN: 978-1-909132-36-8, Pages: 142,
Format: Paperback, Published: 2012
Also available in eBook format!

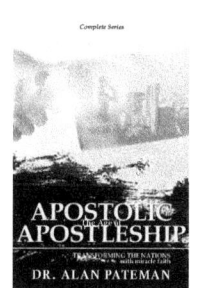

The Age of Apostolic Apostleship
Complete Series

In order to view how the Apostolic baton was successfully passed from one generation to the next. Knowing that through the perseverance and obedience of others - history as we know it was altered forever. Dr. Alan Pateman, a modern day apostle (ascension) looks to reflect on their testimony in this wonderful book.

ISBN: 978-1-909132-65-8, Pages: 420
Format: Paperback, Published: 2017
Also available in eBook format!

ALAN PATEMAN WORLD MISSIONS.COM

Join us in Supporting the

GOSPEL

and the work and ministry of

Alan & Jennifer Pateman

BECOME A PATRON

FOR JUST €12 A MONTH

THANK YOU
FOR YOUR CONTINUOUS SUPPORT, WE ARE FAMILY

Patrons Benefits:
1) Patrons monthly news letter
2) Personal mentoring with Dr. Alan through WhatsApp and Prayer
3) Free Book every year
4) Teaching Courses for personal study
5) Free Conference every year
6) Free Patrons Dinner   Tel: 0039 366 329 1315
          ... for those who are Hungry to be Empowered

All Books Available

at

APMI PUBLICATIONS

Email: publications@alanpatemanworldmissions.com
*Also Available from Amazon.com
and other retail outlets.*

*If you purchased this book through Amazon.com
or other and enjoyed reading it, or perhaps one of
my other books, I would be grateful if you could
take a couple of minutes to write a Customer
Review, many thanks.*

BY DR. ALAN PATEMAN

BY DR. JENNIFER PATEMAN

AVAILABLE FROM APMI PUBLICATIONS, AMAZON.COM AND OTHER RETAIL OUTLETS

www.ingramcontent.com/pod-product-compliance
Lightning Source LLC
Chambersburg PA
CBHW071540040426
42452CB00008B/1072